The Laugharne Rivals

Williams Bros

&

Ebsworth Bros

By Vernon Morgan

The Laugharne Rivals

Published by Vernon Morgan Books

September 2022

ISBN: 978-0-9574045-8-8

© Copyright Vernon Morgan (2022)

Other titles published by the same author:

James of Ammanford.	(The history of J. James & Sons Ltd, Ammanford).
SWT 100.	(The South Wales Transport Co. Ltd, centenary).
Images of Old Llanelli & District.	(Historical views of Llanelli & District).
Saml. Eynon & Sons, 'The Hero' Trimsaran.	(The history of Samuel Eynon & Sons).
Silcox Motor Coach Co Ltd, Pembroke Dock.	(The history of Silcox Motor Coach Co. Ltd).
Davies Bros (Pencader) Ltd.	(A history of the Davies Bros. group of companies).
Rees & Williams Ltd, and West Wales Motors Ltd. 'The Friendly Rivals'.	(A history of both companies).
Ffoshelig Coaches Ltd. Carmarthen.	(The history and centenary of Ffoshelig Coaches Ltd).

Cover Picture: This splendid view of Williams Bros.' Albion 'Venturer' CX19, **FCY 766**, fitted with Metro-Cammell H30/26F, 7ft 6inch wide bodywork, was taken in August 1968. It was new to United Welsh Services, Swansea (966), in December 1948, and arrived in Laugharne, January 1962. It was captured here, reversing off the forecourt of Market Lane garage, into Wogan St., Laugharne, after receiving probably its last wash. It was withdrawn the following month, and 6 months later ended up in a Cardiff scrap yard. It could have been an excellent restoration project. *(John Bennett).*

Rear Cover: Ebsworth Bros. Laugharne, purchased this Leyland 'Titan' PD2/1, GBX 808, with Leyland L27/26R 'Low-bridge' type bodywork, new in May 1951, and is seen here loading up at Lammas St, Carmarthen, for the 85 minute journey to Tenby. Unfortunately, Ebsworth Bros. found themselves in financial difficulties in 1954, after buying too many new vehicles, which resulted in their financier and director, Julian Hodge of Cardiff, selling the business to Western Welsh Omnibus Co., to re-coupe his money. This particular vehicle, became f/n 982 in the Western Welsh fleet in December 1954, and was withdrawn by them in 1963. *(The Bus Archive).*

Title Page: Entrepreneur and founder of the Williams Bros. enterprise, Alderman Tudor Williams. *(Author's collection).*

AUTHORS ACKNOWLEDGEMENTS

This publication is dedicated to my dear wife Kathleen, who sadly passed away after a very lengthy illness, in May this year, as the draft to this book was being compiled.

Kath was always very supportive of my transport interests, and typeset my first publication before she became ill. She also accompanied me on visits to bus depots, transport events, and various archives up and down the country. I will miss her dearly after 51 years.

Long before I met Kath, I was introduced to the fleet of Williams Brothers, 'Pioneer Buses', at the age of 14, when I travelled from Carmarthen to Pendine, aboard their 1938 AEC Regent double-deck bus, for my very first holiday, 7 days camping at Pendine, in July 1958.

Already a bus enthusiast, I took an avid interest in that fleet, and as always, I have enjoyed researching the company's history, and compiling this issue in my series of publications.

However, I'm again indebted to numerous people for their sincere help in compiling it.

First of all, I would like to single out and thank Mike Taylor, for allowing me access to 'The CBPG Archive', and to the dedicated voluntary staff of 'The Bus Archive' at Walsall, for allowing me access to their extensive collection of material, including photographs.

My sincere thanks go also to fellow bus enthusiasts, John Bennett, John Jones, John Martin, Richard Evans, Simon Nicholas, David Donati, and Elfed Lewis, for their sincere help and encouragement, use of notes, information, documentation and / or photographs.

Thanks also to The Leyland Society, J.I. Thornycroft & Co. Ltd., Alan Broughall, Alan Cross, Robert Edworthy, Robert Mack, Roy Marshall, Don Jones (LTBS), Peter Yeomans, J.S. Cockshot, R.H.G. Simpson, Geoff Morant, M.G. Collingdon, D.S. Giles, Georgina & Ian John, Winston John, and Eric Wain, for use of their photographs.

Not forgetting the information and material supplied by Arwel Jones, proprietor of the coach business, 'Jones of Login', and to Laugharne residents, Peter Jenkins, James & Joan Griffiths, together with Laugharne newsletter editor, Denize McIntyre, and the family of the late Clem Thomas, for use of notes from his publication.

Much other valuable information has come from material in the care of Carmarthenshire County Council Cultural Services Department, The PSV Circle, and the 'Welsh Bus & Coach' monthly newsletter.

I must point out that it has not always been possible to identify individual photographers. No discourtesy is intended through lack of acknowledgement, in view of which, I trust they will accept my sincere thanks.

Finally, a big thank you to my daughter, Katie, for her contribution towards this publication. Katie proofread my draft, and corrected small grammatical errors.

CONTENTS

INTRODUCTION

One of the most westerly towns in the county of Carmarthenshire, is the medieval town of Laugharne (Welsh translation, Talacharn), with its roots dating back more than 730 years. The Corporation of Laugharne was granted by charter in 1290, by Sir Guido de Brione.

The Township of Laugharne, with a population of around 2700 in 2019, is situated on the estuary of the River Tâf, and is almost a unique institution, as together with the City of London Corporation, are the last surviving medieval Corporations in the UK.

Laugharne can also boast a connection to the world renowned poet, Dylan Thomas, who fell in love with this historic fishing town in 1934, making it his home from 1949, until his untimely death in New York on 9th November, 1953. On his first visit to Laugharne in 1934, Dylan described the town as remarkable, a timeless, mild, beguiling island of a town, and added that it was 'the strangest town in Wales'.

Besides the town's historic castle dating from the twelfth century, there are 69 listed buildings in the Township, including 'The Castle House', 'Island House', and 'The Great House', which all date from the Tudor period, the Town Hall, and the sixteenth century parish church, 'St Martins', which is the resting place of Dylan Thomas (1914-1953), 'The Boathouse', where Dylan Thomas lived, and his famous 'Writing Shed', not forgetting the 'Brown's Hotel' – Dylan Thomas' favourite drinking haunt.

Throughout the years however, Laugharne has been home to many colourful characters, in fact, too many to mention, but this publication is centred upon just one of those characters, namely, Tudor Hurst Fleming Williams, who was born in the Township of Laugharne, on 29th May, 1891. Tudor was the son of Owen Williams, a local stone mason with nine children – 2 girls and 7 boys. He was the seventh child with 2 younger brothers, and a true 'Laugharney / Laugharnee / Larnie'. (Note: This is a slang word with different spellings).

The name 'Fleming' had been handed down through the family for generations, a name derived from 'Flemish'. Tudor's ancestors on his mother's side of the family originated from the Flemish region of Belgium (Flanders), landing in Laugharne after the Norman invasion, during the 12th century.

In June 1908, at the age of 17, Tudor had the foresight and business acumen to commence a road passenger transport service between Laugharne, and the busy St. Clears Railway Station, using a horse-drawn, six seat wagonette, sometimes called a 'brake', later modernising to the mechanical mode of transport in a partnership with his two younger brothers.

Six months earlier, the Great Western Railway Company had promised the Township, that a motor bus service between Laugharne and St. Clears Railway Station, would commence in May 1908, but Tudor 'pipped them at the post' when the GWR failed to deliver.

Tudor was a real gentleman, who was elected as 'Portreeve' of Laugharne for three consecutive years (1934-1936), and immediately afterwards, became an Alderman. In 1955, he was elected as a County Councillor.

Apart from his sharp and witty mind, Tudor stood out sartorially in a crowd. He wore breeches, highly polished brown boots, and leather leggings, with brass strap buckles shining like mirrors, topped off with an Edwardian brown jacket, with matching shirt and bow tie. The only variation in this immaculate turn-out, was a pair of knee-length puttees, which were wound around a pair of imposing calves with military precision. The whole outfit was stylishly topped off with an imposing Baden-Powell style velour brownish hat.

Tudor was a man of standing. He could be as harsh or as gentle as the occasion demanded. He granted many favours to many people, without thought of reward, and his buses were available to go anywhere, very often for no charge whatsoever. The only stipulation was that you gave the driver a tip.

Alderman Tudor Hurst Fleming Williams can be fondly remembered, standing like a sentry on the cobbled street outside his garage in Market Lane; a truly unforgettable character.

Nevertheless, in order to complete the picture of Williams Brothers' enterprise, it was necessary to include the history of their competitors, Ebsworth Brothers.

The Ebsworth brothers originated from the seaside village of Pendine, five miles west of Laugharne, a village famous for its land speed records. The brothers had a variety of business interests in the community, ranging from game-keeper, game dealer, and butcher, to motor engineers, hotel and garage proprietors, before diversifying into car hire, and expanding into public transport and road haulage. The transport side of their business commenced from the family run Beach Hotel, and Beach Hotel Garage at Pendine, but quickly moved into Laugharne, when John Lewis Ebsworth (Jack Ebsworth), and his brother Tom, moved to Fullerton House, King Street, next door to the famous 'Brown's Hotel'.

The Ebsworth brothers were fortunate enough to meet all the famous racing drivers and record breakers at the Beach Hotel, which is situated alongside the old slipway to Pendine Sands. The record breakers usually stayed at the Beach Hotel on race weekends, using the hotel garage for adjustments, repairs and maintenance.

In 1919, however, a very bitter challenge developed between the Ebsworth brothers, and Tudor Williams and his brothers, which finally ended in December 1954, when the registered company of Ebsworth Brothers Ltd., got into financial difficulties, and their omnibus concern passed to the Western Welsh Omnibus Co. Ltd.

Finally, the spelling of place names referred to in this story are taken from authenticated records of that period in time, as several Welsh place names were changed to the true Welsh spelling from around 1960 onwards.

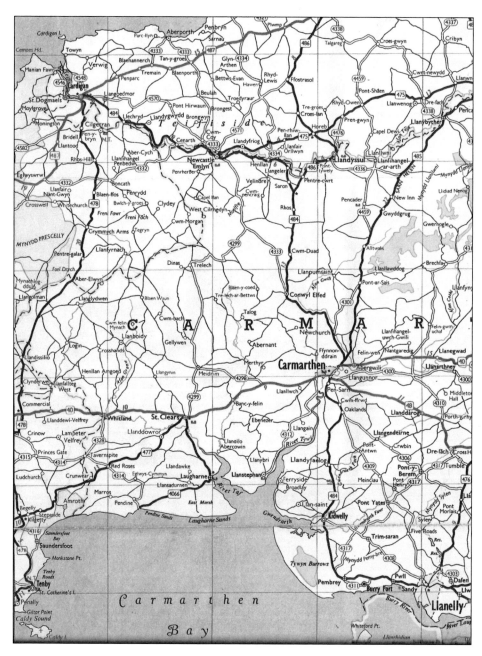

A historic map of west Carmarthenshire showing the location of Laugharne, and the surrounding area mentioned in this story.

HOW TUDOR WILLIAMS' BUSINESS STARTED

'Kelly's Business Directory' of 1895 stated, "There are three public transport conveyers running from St Clears Railway Station, through the town of St Clears, to Laugharne, three times daily, and in summer, extends to Pendine, but not on Sundays'. The carriers were Henry Hitchings and Richard Pearce, both of Frogmore Street, Laugharne, and Evan David, of King Street, Laugharne, who was also listed as a coal merchant, farmer, haulier, 'bus' owner and a parcel agent for the Great Western Railway Company (GWR).

In 1903, however, the GWR began the slow process of introducing feeder bus services to and from their railway stations, a process that didn't reach South Wales for a few years. Nevertheless, it was five years later in January 1908, when the GWR finally announced their intention to start a motor bus service in May 1908, from St. Clears Railway Station to Pendine, via Laugharne - which would be their headquarters. The service never materialised.

The GWR's failure to provide the promised service, prompted 17 year old Tudor Hurst Fleming Williams to start a passenger service with a horse-drawn six seat wagonette, sometimes called a 'brake', between Laugharne and the busy St. Clears Railway Station, five miles north of Laugharne. The service was timed to meet the busy trains on the Great Western Railway's London to Fishguard, and London to Pembroke routes.

Above: This Wagonette and two horses pictured in Laugharne, is thought to be one of Tudor Williams'. *(C.J. Taylor Archive).*

9

In 1971, Tudor Williams confirmed that his passenger service from Laugharne to St Clears Railway Station commenced 5th June 1908, from 'The Mews' at Market Lane, Laugharne, correcting an error printed in Garkes' Directory, which had given the date as June 1907.

Tudor's business venture was very successful, and in 1913, he obtained the Post Office mail carrier's contract for Laugharne, later acquiring a 'coach and four' for the contract, which gave him the title of 'coachman'.

June 1914, saw the arrival of Tudor Williams' first motor vehicle, a green and yellow Humber 10/12hp registered BX 448, but soon afterwards in September 1914, came the outbreak of WW1, when the horses were commandeered by the Army for use by the country's troops. At that point, things looked very bleak for Tudor, but in order to continue running his service, he bought two Ford 'Model T' motor cars, registered DE 899, and BX 672, in April 1915 and February 1916 respectively. He used all his petrol rations, and 'borrowed' petrol from the family doctor in order to survive.

In the meantime, the well renowned business entrepreneurs, Ebsworth Brothers of Pendine, could see how well Tudor was doing with his transport business, which prompted them to compete against him, shortly after the cessation of World War 1 hostilities. There are unconfirmed reports stating that "they would run Tudor off the road".

The history of Ebsworth brothers' businesses is dealt with separately on pages 131 to 191.

Tudor's 'Model T' saloons were used continuously until after war ended, and when the business started to build up again in 1919, he bought a variety of cheap government surplus vehicles. He acquired a second-hand 'Napier' chassis (built by D. Napier & Sons Ltd, at Acton Vale, West London), and fitted it with a charabanc body, registered BX 958 in June 1919. Afterwards, a Dennis chassis arrived, which Tudor and Ben Tucker bodied themselves with a 32 seat bus body, and a Talbot ambulance, which he converted into a 10 seat bus, together with a new Ford 'Model T' brake, BX 937, and a Ford 'Model TT' lorry BX 968, which was converted into a charabanc. Soon afterwards came a Ford 'Model T' Landaulette registered BX 1005, and another Ford 'Model TT' with bus bodywork, registered BX 1078.

Left: Not a brilliant photograph, but in consideration, this picture was taken 115 years ago. This was Tudor Williams' first wagonette, which was built by the famous coachbuilder, Hooper's of Westminster, London. The view appears to have been taken outside 'The Mews' in Market Lane, Laugharne.

TUDOR WILLIAMS & BROTHERS (PIONEER BUSES)

When the Ebsworth brothers began their challenge against Tudor Williams in 1919, his two younger brothers, Ebie and William joined the business, which was listed in Kelly's Business Directory of 1920, as 'Tudor Williams & Brothers, The Garage, Market Lane, Laugharne, motor car and charabanc operators'. The garage in Market Lane had previously been Tudor Williams' Mews, and was converted into a garage to accommodate and maintain the cars and buses.

The Ebsworth brothers apparently gave Tudor a tough time, but he retaliated, and equally gave them a tough time too. The main issues of the rivalry are all recorded within this story.

Tudor's newly formed partnership bought another Ford 'TT' in April 1920, registered BX 1224. This one had detachable charabanc, and lorry bodies, and was followed by a left hand drive 'American' Dodge, purchased at the Bath & West Show a few months later.

In 1921, another former war department bus was purchased from the 'WD dump' in Slough. This was a 30hp Thornycroft 'J' with 20 seats, which was registered BX 1953, and lettered with their short lived fleet-name, 'Laugharne Motor Service'. A few months later, there was another arrival, a Fiat 18BL registered BX 3128, which Tudor bodied himself.

Above: This view of **BX 1953**, a former War Department Thornycroft 'J', troop carrier, was taken outside Morgan's Garage at Pendine, when Tudor Williams & Brothers were using the fleetname Laugharne Motor Service. That fleetname was quickly dropped, in favour of 'Pioneer'. Tudor Williams is the gentleman on the left, holding his infant son, Tudor Evelyn Williams "Tudie", who was born February 1920. *(V. Morgan collection).*

11

Above: An interesting photograph of the rival operators' buses parked together at St Clears Railway Station in 1925. The vehicle parked on the left is reputedly an 'Oldsmobile' of Ebsworth Bros. **BX 235**, which is either a re-issued registration mark, or it has one number missing, i.e: **BX 235?** There are no records available to check this issue. The vehicle on the right is Tudor Williams Bros.' Fiat 18BL, **BX 3128**, with primitive bodywork built by Tudor Williams. *(Peter Jenkins, collection).*

In comparison with other local authorities, Carmarthen Borough Council were late implementing their hackney licensing obligations. Discussions regarding bus control in the county town, had been held frequently between 1924 and 1926, but the first licences were not issued until February 1926.

There is no evidence of Williams Bros. or Ebsworth Bros., plying into Carmarthen before that date. It appears that both were happily fighting over the service between Pendine and St Clears Railway Station, where their clientele caught trains to Carmarthen and elsewhere.

However, Williams Bros. received their first Hackney licence from the Carmarthen authority on 24th February, 1926, for a vehicle registered BX 6301 to ply into the town, with their terminus at Guildhall Square. At the same time, it was stated that all bus operators would have to come to a satisfactory arrangement regarding their timetables, otherwise the council would arrange them.

Four months later, Williams Bros. were granted a Saturday service between Carmarthen and Llangunnock (Llangynog), and Sunday journeys on the Carmarthen to Pendine route, and in October 1926, asked to run addition weekday journeys between Carmarthen and Pendine.

In the meantime however, competitors Ebsworth Bros. developed close links with Green's Motors of Haverfordwest, when Green's briefly ran a service from Tenby to Carmarthen, via Pendine, Laugharne, and St. Clears in 1926. Green's Motors garaged those buses at Ebsworth Bros.' Central Garage premises, and loaned Ebsworth Bros. a spare bus in July 1926, when one of theirs was off the road due to maintenance issues.

On 19th April, 1927, Carmarthen B.C. licensing committee invited all bus proprietors plying into Carmarthen, to attend a meeting regarding the "unacceptable state of affairs". They were asked to co-operate with the 'Watch Committee' to improve services, otherwise steps would be taken. Licences were then issued to all applicants for a one month period only, and monthly thereafter. At this meeting, Ebsworth Bros. were granted their first 'official' licence to ply into Carmarthen, but knowing the past history of Ebsworth Bros. and Tudor Williams Bros., the licensing committee specified that in order to prevent racing between them, the service timings of 9.00 and 9.30 am daily, would be shared equally, by running it on alternate weeks. Two weeks later however, they decided to licence both operators, and to give them warnings of the consequences if they did not adhere to their conditions and timetables.

Nevertheless, the inevitable soon happened. The council's 'Watch Committee' reported on 29th June, 1927, that Ebsworth Brothers were not running in accordance with their timetable, and that there were complaints of abusive conduct from their drivers towards the rival service. They were also running Carmarthen to Llangunnock (Llangynog), which was not authorised. At the meeting, the licensing committee decided to revoke Ebsworth Brothers' three Hackney licences, and the authorisation to operate Ebsworth Brothers' share of the Carmarthen to Pendine service, be given to Tudor Williams Brothers.

A week later, the licensing committee held a special meeting, where Ebsworth Brothers gave an undertaking that they would comply with the committee's requirements, and were prepared to run their service according to a timetable *previously* granted to Green's Motors, for their erstwhile Tenby - Pendine - Carmarthen route, and stated they would comply with any other requirements. Two hackney licences were immediately reinstated with conditions, and a month later, on 27th July, 1927, the third licence was reinstated, along with a licence for the Carmarthen to Llangunnock route.

Nevertheless, the rivalry continued, and it was Tudor Williams Brothers' turn to have a warning from Carmarthen B.C. licensing committee for irregular running on 27th July, 1927.

A year later in June 1928, Tudor Williams Brothers asked the Carmarthen and Tenby B.C. licensing authorities for a licence to operate a service between those two towns. The licence was granted by both authorities a fortnight later in July 1928.

At this point in time, the GWR were eager to expand their network of services, and applied to Carmarthen B.C. on 14th November, 1928, for three 'new' licences, Carmarthen to Pendine, Carmarthen to Pencader, and Carmarthen to Narberth. The licensing committee refused all three routes, as they were already sufficiently covered by other operators.

With regards to the Carmarthen – Narberth service, via St Clears and Whitland, it was a service already established by Benjamin Davies, of County Supply Stores, St Clears, which was running jointly with W. Edwards & Sons, (the Ford car dealers), Towy Garage, Carmarthen, from 1st November, 1928. This service competed to an extent against Williams Bros. and Ebsworth Bros. on the road between Carmarthen and St Clears.

Carmarthen, Narberth and Whitland 'Bus Service

Has been taken over by

W. EDWARDS & SONS,

Towy Garage, CARMARTHEN,

Who will run the latest and most up-to-date 'Buses, one of which has just arrived from the Glasgow Show

Passengers are assured of every comfort and attention on this service.

Any suggestions for improvemet will be gladly welcomed

Above: This announcement for W. Edwards & Sons' bus service, appeared in a local newspaper dated November 1928.

Below: A selection of bus tickets used by W. Edwards & Sons, with advertisements on the back for their motor garage.

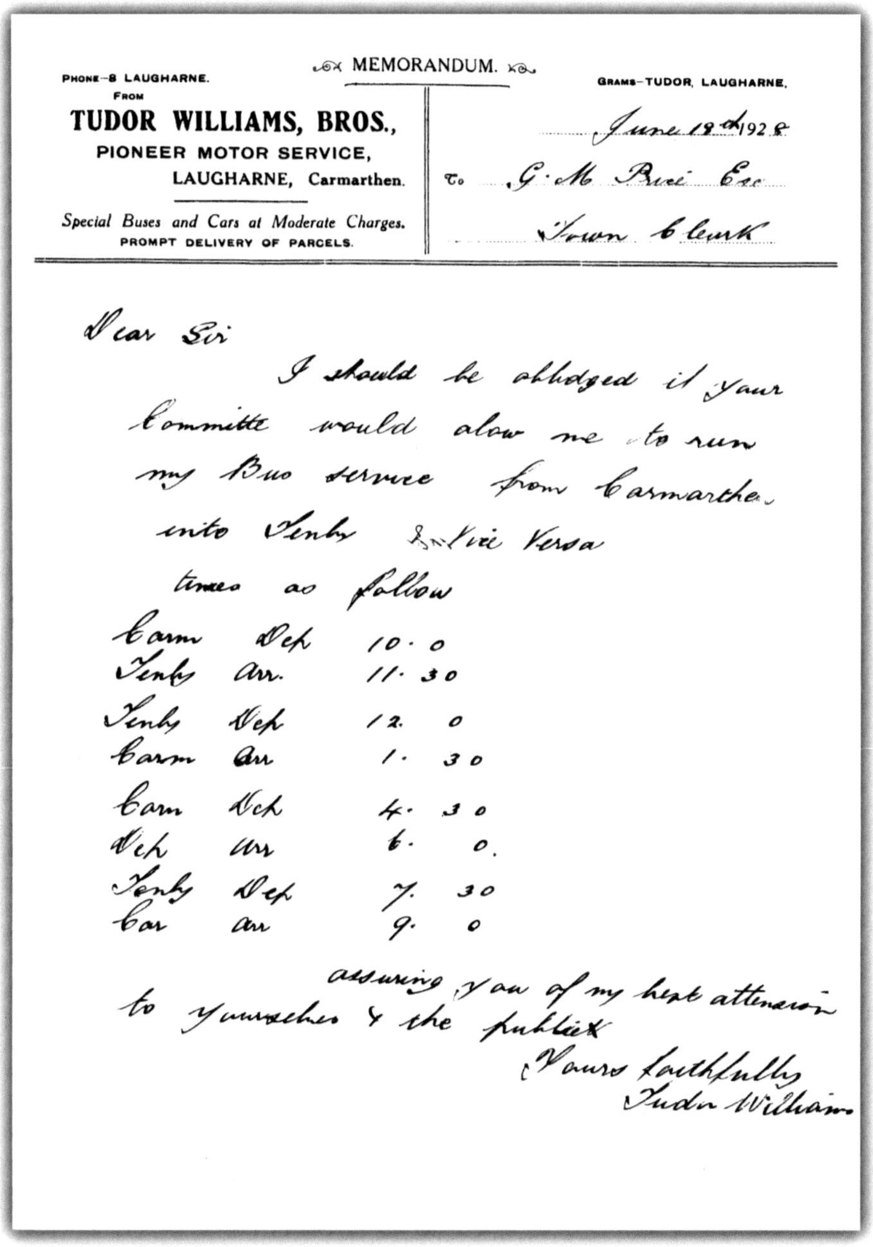

PHONE—8 LAUGHARNE.

✦ MEMORANDUM. ✦

GRAMS—TUDOR, LAUGHARNE.

FROM

TUDOR WILLIAMS, BROS.,
PIONEER MOTOR SERVICE,
LAUGHARNE, Carmarthen.

Special Buses and Cars at Moderate Charges.
PROMPT DELIVERY OF PARCELS.

June 19th 1928

To *G. M. Price Esq*

Town Clerk

Dear Sir

I should be obliged if your Committee would alow me to run my Bus service from Carmarthen into Tenby & Vice Versa

times as follow

Carm	Dep	10 . 0
Tenby	Arr.	11 . 30
Tenby	Dep	12 . 0
Carm	Arr	1 . 30
Carm	Dep	4 . 30
Dep	Arr	6 . 0 .
Tenby	Dep	7 . 30
Car	Arr	9 . 0

assuring you of my best attention to yourselves & the public

Yours faithfully
Tudor William

<u>Above:</u> The timetable Tudor Williams submitted to Tenby B.C. in his application for a Carmarthen to Tenby service in 1928.

Form R.F.8. (Revised August, 1925.)

This Form must be used for one Vehicle only. When completed it must be sent and duty paid to the Taxation Department of the Local Authority of the District in which the Vehicle is ordinarily kept. (The address can be obtained by enquiry at a Post Office).

This form must not be used for renewal of a licence unless the Vehicle has changed hands since the last licence was issued.

☞ **FILL IN THE YEAR.**   **YEAR 192 .**

Declaration for a Licence and Application for Registration of a

MECHANICALLY-PROPELLED HACKNEY VEHICLE (other than a Motor Cycle.)

(If you have more than six HACKNEY Vehicles OF UNIFORM TYPE use Form R.F.8A. This Form R.F.8 is not to be used for vehicles not described above.)

A.—APPLICATION.

I apply for a licence for a :—

MOTOR HACKNEY VEHICLE:—

Seating capacity (exclusive of driver) calculated according to Definition F. (2) overleaf :—

	Annual Licences expiring on 31st December.		Quarterly Licences*		Amount to pay.
	Full Duty †	EXPIRING (say whether 24th March, 30th June, 30th Sept. or 31st Dec.)	Full Duty †		
	£ s. d.	£ s. d.	£ s. d.	£ s. d.	
Not more than 6 persons	{ 15 0 / 12 0		{ 4 2 6 / 3 6 0		
More than 6 but not more than 14 persons	{ 30 0 / 24 0	24 3 26	{ 8 5 0 / 6 12 0	2 4	
More than 14 but not more than 20 persons	{ 45 0 / 36 0		{ 12 7 6 / 9 18 0		
More than 20 but not more than 26 persons	{ 60 0 / 48 0		{ 16 10 0 / 13 4 0		
More than 26 but not more than 32 persons	{ 72 0 / 60 0		{ 19 16 0 / 16 10 0		
More than 32 persons	{ 84 0 / 70 0		{ 23 2 0 / 19 5 0		

NOTE.—The higher rates are payable for Hackney vehicles which are licensed (or to be licensed) to ply for hire, and for vehicles to be let for hire, within the Metropolitan Police District as defined by the Metropolitan Public Carriage Act, 1869 (32 & 33 Vict., cap. 115) or other Area (if any) scheduled by the Minister of Transport.

*Quarterly Licences for Motor Hackneys are granted on payment of 27½ per cent. of the full annual duty for the periods January 1st to March 24th; March 25th to June 30th; July 1st to September 30th; or October 1st to December 31st. †Licences are also granted for periods other than annual or quarterly; for scales of duty see back of form.

B.   **PARTICULARS OF MOTOR HACKNEY VEHICLE.**

(a) Has the vehicle been previously registered under the Roads Act, 1920 ?   *No*

If not :—
(i) Is it a new vehicle ?   *Yes*
If so, evidence of this such as the Manufacturer's or an accredited Agent's Sales Delivery Note, Invoice or the like, should be supplied

(ii) If not a new vehicle, a satisfactory explanation must be supplied as to why it has not been previously registered   *Trevor Hopkins Carmarthen*

(b) Registered Mark and Number (if any)   *BX 6626*

(c) Type of body   *Bus*
(If alternative bodies are kept for use, particulars of each Type should be given)   *—*

(d) Colour   *Red & White*
(If alternative bodies are kept for use the colour of each should be given)

(e) Manufacturer's
{ Name   *Chevrolet*
{ Description of Vehicle   *RT 2100162*
{ Chassis Type Letter and Number.   *MO*

(f) Year of Manufacture of Engine (if known)   *1926*   Horse-power   *23*

(g) Engine Number.   *RT2100162*

(h) If Internal combustion engine, give—
{ Number of { a Single Piston   cylinders having { Two Pistons   *4*
{ Internal diameter of cylinders.

(i) Seating capacity (exclusive of driver)   *14 Seats*
See definition F. (2) overleaf

(j) Weight of vehicle unladen   *1 10 0 0*
See definition F. (3) overleaf

If the Unladen Weight is upwards of 2 tons, the following additional details are required :—

(k) Axle-weights (laden) { Front   as defined in the Heavy   Motor Car Order, 1904 { Rear

(l) Diameter of Wheels { Front   { Rear

(m) Width of Tyres { Front ... Inches. { Rear ... Inches.

(n) Material of Tyres

C.—DECLARATION.

I Declare that I am a Person whose business it is to sell Vehicles or let Vehicles for Hire and that the foregoing Declaration for a Licence and Application for Registration contains a full and true account of the particulars which the Law requires me to state, and that the Vehicle is ordinarily kept by me at......

I further declare that the vehicle has not been or will not be used by me between the date of expiration of the last licence and the date of commencement of the licence for which application is now made.

The words within the brackets [ ] should be deleted if the vehicle has not previously been licensed, or if the application is for a licence for a period immediately following the period covered by the last licence.

In the case of limited liability companies the name and address of the registered office of the Company should be given and the declaration should be signed by the Managing Director or the Secretary. In the case of a private firm the name by which it is ordinarily known should be given, and the names of the partners together with the signature of one of the partners. If this Declaration is signed by an agent or steward

USUAL SIGNATURE   *Tudor Williams*

NAME IN FULL (IN BLOCK CAPITALS.)   *Tudor Williams*
ADDRESS   *The Garage Laugharne*

<u>**Above:**</u> Motor Taxation form for the company's 14 seat Chevrolet, **BX 6626** dated 10/3/1926.   *(Courtesy of CTPG).*

☛ **FILL IN THE YEAR.**   **YEAR 192_._** .

Declaration for a Licence and Application for Registration of a
MECHANICALLY-PROPELLED HACKNEY VEHICLE (other than a Motor Cycle.)
(If you have more than six HACKNEY Vehicles OF UNIFORM TYPE use Form R.F.8A. This Form R.F.8 is not to be used for vehicles not described above.)

A.—APPLICATION.

I apply for a licence for the period commencing............*1st May*.........192_._
and ending............*30 June*............192_8_, for a :—

VEHICLE being a Hackney Carriage as defined in section four of the Customs and Inland Revenue Act, 1888 :—

Seating capacity (exclusive of driver) calculated according to Note E. (4) overleaf :—

	Annual Licences expiring on 31st December.		Quarterly Licences.			Amount to pay.		
	Full Duty.		Full Duty.*					
	£	s.	£	s.	d.	£	s.	d.
Not more than 8 persons	15	0	4	2	6			
More than 8 but not more than 14 persons	30	0	8	5	0	*5*	*10*	
More than 14 but not more than 20 persons	45	0	12	7	6			
More than 20 but not more than 26 persons	60	0	16	10	0			
More than 26 but not more than 32 persons	72	0	19	16	0			
More than 32 but not more than 40 persons	84	0	23	2	0			
More than 40 but not more than 48 persons	96	0	26	8	0			
More than 48 but not more than 56 persons	108	0	29	14	0			
More than 56 but not more than 64 persons	120	0	33	0	0			
Additional for each person in excess of 64	1	10		8	3			

Quarterly Licences for Motor Hackneys are granted on payment of 27½ per cent. of the full annual duty for the periods January 1st to March 24th ; March 25th to June 30th ; July 1st to September 30th ; or October 1st to December 31st.
*Licences are also granted for periods other than annual or quarterly ; for scales of duty see back of form.

B.   **PARTICULARS OF MOTOR HACKNEY VEHICLE.**

(a) Has the vehicle been previously registered under the Roads Act, 1920 ? *No*

If not :—
(i) Is it a new vehicle ? *Yes*
If so, evidence of this such as the Manufacturer's or an accredited Agent's Sales Delivery Note, Invoice or the like, should be supplied *McOurd*
(ii) If not a new vehicle, a satisfactory explanation must be supplied as to why it has not been previously registered *Nelson Garage*

(b) Registered Mark and Number (if any) *BX 8740 Bus.*

(c) Type of body *Bus*
(If alternative bodies are kept for use, particulars of each Type should be given)

(d) Colour *Purple & Cream*
(If alternate bodies are kept for use the colour of each should be given)

(e) Manufacturer's :
Name *GMC*
Description of Vehicle *Bus*
Chassis Type Letter and Number *T.20*
Horse-power *28*

(f) Number of Engine *20387°*

(g) If Internal combustion engine, give :—
Number of cylinders having { Single Piston { Two Pistons *Internal combustion*
Internal diameter of cylinders *4 cylinder*

(h) Seating capacity (exclusive of driver) *14*
See Note E. (4) overleaf

(i) Is the body of the vehicle specially constructed to provide space for standing passengers ? *Yes*

(j) Weight of vehicle unladen *1 16 0 0*
See deduction F. (2) overleaf

If the Unladen Weight exceeds 2 tons, give the following additional particulars :—

(k) Axle-weights (laden) as defined in the Heavy Motor Car Order, 1904 Front..... Middle..... Rear.....

(l) Diameter of Wheels Front..... Middle..... Rear.....

(m) Width of Tyres Front..... Middle..... Rear.....

(n) Type of Tyres (State whether pneumatic, solid rubber or metal.)

C.—DECLARATION.

I Declare that I am a Person whose business it is to sell Vehicles or let Vehicles for Hire and that the foregoing Declaration for a Licence and Application for Registration contains a full and true account of the particulars which the Law requires me to state, and that the Vehicle is ordinarily kept by me at............
[I further declare that the vehicle has not been or will not be used by me between the date of expiration of the last licence and the date of commencement of the licence for which application is now made.]
[The words within the brackets [ ] should be deleted if the vehicle has not previously been licensed, or if the application is for a licence for a period immediately following the expiration of the last licence.
In the case of limited liability companies the name and address of the registered office of the Company should be given and the declaration should be signed by the Managing Director or the Secretary.
In the case of a private firm the name by which it is ordinarily known should be given, and the names of the partners together with the signature of one of the partners.
If this Declaration is signed by an agent or steward the fact must be clearly indicated, and the full name and address of both principal or employer, and that of the agent or steward must be inserted.

USUAL SIGNATURE *Tudor Williams*
NAME IN FULL (IN BLOCK CAPITALS) *Tudor Williams*
ADDRESS *Garage, Langham, Carmarthen*
DATE............192......

[P.T.O.

[DO NOT WRITE] [CLIMATE C. 17 MAY 1928 LICENCE]

Above: Motor Taxation form for the company's 14 seat GMC T20, **BX 8740** dated 17/5/1928. *(Courtesy of CTPG).*

17

On 8th April, 1929, Tudor Williams Bros. and Ebsworth Bros. were successful in gaining one extra Hackney licence each from the Carmarthen licensing authority, increasing their authorisation to four licences each. A week later on 16th April, Tudor Williams asked the Carmarthen licensing committee for continuance of their Carmarthen to Tenby licence, stating, *"Hoping to run to your satisfaction. We will run in winter if issued"*.

However, on 21st December, 1929, the Tenby B.C. gave Tudor an unwelcome Christmas present. They wrote to inform him that he had not complied with council regulations, and were revoking one vehicle licence (Hackney licence).

The partnership ignored their warning, and in March 1930, had their road service licence revoked by Tenby B.C., having contravened their licence obligations, i.e. Neglecting their winter services, amongst other compliances.

Ebsworth Bros. heard about Williams Bros.' misfortunes, and immediately applied for a licence to operate the route, submitting applications to Tenby and Carmarthen councils on 8th March, 1930. The licence was granted by both authorities, for continuance of the service by means of the same route and timetable.

PHONE—8 LAUGHARNE.
FROM

⚡ MEMORANDUM. ⚡

GRAMS—TUDOR, LAUGHARNE

Laugharne Electric Supply,
Proprietors —TUDOR WILLIAMS BROS.,
LAUGHARNE, Carmarthen.

Batteries Charged and all Electric Equipments Stocked.

May 11th 192 9

To The Town Clerk.

Tenby.

Dear Sir –

I shall be much obliged to you if you will put my application - which I left with your Clerk last Monday - before your next Meeting which I understand is next Monday.

Yours faithfully
Tudor Williams.

Above: Tudor Williams wrote this letter to Tenby B.C. on 11th May, 1929, using a letterhead from the partnership's subsidiary business, 'Laugharne Electric Supply'. Tudor Williams Brothers, generated electricity at their engine house opposite Market Lane garage, and supplied the whole township with electricity in those far gone days. *(C.J. Taylor archive).*

Interestingly, in February 1930, Western Welsh Omnibus Co., the reformed Great Western Railway bus company, purchased the Carmarthen to Narberth route, via St Clears and Whitland from the joint operators of the service, Benjamin Davies of St Clears, and Wm. Edwards & Sons, of Towy Garage, Carmarthen, and in April 1930, the Carmarthen licensing committee granted Western Welsh a modification to that licence, allowing an extension beyond Narberth to reach Tenby, via Templeton. Tenby B.C. similarly granted Western Welsh permission for the licence.

Consequently, in April 1930, Tudor Williams gave reasons for the neglect of his winter services and compliances, and asked Tenby Council to reconsider their decision. At the same time, he provided evidence that he did not pick up passengers on D.J. Morrison's section of route between Tenby and Kilgetty, and vice versa. The council then reinstated his licence, albeit on a different timetable.

This was a recipe for disaster, and in June 1930, Ebsworth Bros. reported to Tenby Council that Williams Brothers were running irregularly. They allegedly stated that Williams Brothers were running on *their* Carmarthen to Tenby times on 14/15/16/19/20th & 23rd May, and they did not operate the service at all on 17/21/23/24//26th May. They also stated that Williams Brothers were not leaving Tenby, in accordance with their timetable in the evenings.

Tenby Council decided to ask Williams Bros. for an explanation, and to alter the scheduled evening leaving times of Ebsworth Bros. and Williams Bros.

A letter was sent to Tudor Williams Bros. on 2nd July, 1930, stating 'You have not adhered to your timetable. If there are any more issues, we will deal with the matter severely'.

Williams Bros. persisted in running irregularly, and as a result, the Tenby B.C. licensing committee sent out licence renewal notices to all operators *except* Tudor Williams Bros., on 1st August, 1930, inviting them to renew their licences for the forthcoming year.

In addition to that, when the Road Traffic Act 1930 was implemented in April 1931, Tenby B.C. decided to oppose any application Williams Bros. made to the Traffic Commissioners, for a Carmarthen to Tenby road service licence, provided that the opposing bus operators, D.J. Morrison, and Ebsworth Bros., pay the council's expenses in the matter.

The arrangement was agreed upon by the opposing operators, resulting in the new licensing authority, the Ministry of Transport's Traffic Commissioners, rejecting Williams Bros.' application for a Carmarthen to Tenby road service licence (TGR 457/1), as seen on the next page.

EFFECTS OF THE ROAD TRAFFIC ACT 1930

The next major event in the company's history was The Road Traffic Act 1930, which became a 'Godsend' to most operators, but was not the case for Tudor Williams and his brothers.

This Act of Parliament, which was passed in August 1930, gave the Ministry of Transport's Traffic Commissioners full control of public service vehicles (PSVs), together with passenger services and their licensing in Great Britain.

These Traffic Commissioners, with the power vested in them, brought about improved operating conditions, adherence to timetables, and stability of fares. All stage carriage and express service routes had to be licensed, and the granting of such licences, which had previously been under the jurisdiction of the local authorities, were then only obtainable through the Ministry of Transport's Traffic Commissioners. Licences to drive and conduct a PSV also became the Traffic Commissioners responsibility. Under this new licensing system, all PSV operators were issued with operator identification numbers, by which they were identified. Consequently, the number issued to Tudor Williams Brothers, was TGR 457, with each road service licence applied for thereafter, given licence application numbers beginning with the operator identification number.

After implementing the new Traffic Act fully, in April 1931, every bus and coach operator had to re-apply to the new authority for renewal of each licence held, and re-apply annually thereafter. Likewise, any changes to services, times, fares, or new routes, all had to be applied for, and the licences would only be granted when approved by the Traffic Commissioners. However, the first licences Tudor Williams Brothers applied for under the new Act in April 1931, were licences for services which they claimed to have operated for the previous year:-

TGR 457/1   **Carmarthen (Guildhall Square)** to **Tenby (South Parade).**
via: Bankyfelin, St Clears, Red Roses, Llanteg, Stepaside and Kilgetty.
Objections received from Ebsworth Bros., D.J. Morrison, and Tenby B.C.
After a public hearing, the licence was refused 10/1931.

TGR 457/2   **Carmarthen (Guildhall Square)** to **Pendine.**
via: Bankyfelin, St Clears, and Laugharne.
This licence was granted on 29/9/1931, with the following conditions:-
[1] The part of the service between Laugharne and Pendine shall be run between 1ˢᵗ June and 30ᵗʰ September only, or any other such period as the Traffic Commissioners decide.
[2] The licensee shall be entitled to run a duplicate bus on Wednesdays & Saturdays, leaving Carmarthen at 4.15pm, 8pm, and 10pm.
[3] The service is to be operated jointly with Ebsworth Bros.

TGR 457/3   Carmarthen (Guildhall Square) to Llangunnock (Llangynog).
via: Johnstown and Sarnau.
This licence was granted on 25/11/1931, with the following condition:-
[1] The service is to be run on Saturdays, and days when Fairs and Marts
are held in Carmarthen.

It appears that Tudor Williams forgot to apply for renewal of their 'pioneering' service between St Clears Railway Station and Pendine, as it appeared in 'Notices & Proceedings' dated 12th August, 1931, as a *'new'* application for stage carriage service:-

TGR 457/4   St Clears (Railway Station) to Pendine.
via: Laugharne.
This licence was granted on 29/9/1931, with the following condition:-
[1] The part of the service between Laugharne and Pendine shall be run
between 1ˢᵗ June and 30ᵗʰ September only.

In the meantime, Tudor Williams Bros. objected to all three licence renewals submitted by Ebsworth Bros. on 25ᵗʰ March, 1931, resulting in Ebsworth Bros. losing their share of the St Clears Railway Station to Pendine service, but were granted renewal of Carmarthen to Tenby, and joint operation of Carmarthen to Pendine, shared with Williams Brothers.

Above: A superb publicity photograph of **CG 605**, a Thornycroft 'Cygnet' CDF/RC6, with Strachan DP35F bodywork, which Tudor Williams Bros. purchased in April 1932. This was a former Thornycroft demonstrator, built in 1931, and exhibited at the 1931 Commercial Motor Show, but not licenced until February 1932. Originally fitted with a petrol engine, returning a fuel consumption of 5 mpg, it was retrofitted with a diesel engine by Thornycroft, which shook itself to pieces. *(Thornycroft & Co)*.

Above: This rear off-side view of the Thonycroft 'Cygnet', **CG 605**, shows that its emergency door was positioned towards the front end of its front entrance bodywork. Surely this layout was a fire trap, especially on a vehicle fitted with a petrol engine. The livery of this vehicle and all others from the period was given as Blue, Black and Cream. *(J.I. Thornycroft & Co).*

A year later in February 1932, when Tudor Williams Bros. and Ebsworth Bros. applied for annual renewal of their Carmarthen to Pendine road service licences, Western Welsh submitted an objection, which resulted in a public inquiry on 5th October, 1932. In retaliation, Williams Bros. and Ebsworth Bros. submitted objections to Western Welsh's applications for renewal of their Carmarthen to Tenby (TGR 441/46), and Narberth to Haverfordwest licences (TGR 441/86). However, all the licences were granted.

Ebsworth Bros. made another complaint to the Traffic Commissioners in the summer of 1933, stating that Williams Bros. were not running in accordance to their timetable on the Carmarthen to Pendine service, and charging fares below the agreed registered amount.

A public inquiry regarding the issue, chaired by Traffic Commissioner, Mr. A.T. James (KC), was held at Carmarthen's Guildhall on 4th October, 1933, where it was decided that both operators had an agreed fare table and timetable, with interavailable return tickets. Tudor Williams, senior partner of Williams Bros. was reprimanded in court, and his company had their stage carriage service licence for the Carmarthen to Pendine route (TGR 457/2), suspended for 4 weeks, from Monday 9th October, to Sunday 5th November, 1933.

The Traffic Commissioner decided that in order to not inconvenience the travelling public, Western Welsh would run Williams Bros.' share of the service during the suspension period.

Western Welsh were issued with the following short period licences in order to operate Tudor Williams Bros.' service, with the same special conditions:-

TGR 441/Sp/60   Carmarthen to Laugharne, period of operation: 9 - 15 October, 1933.
TGR 441/Sp/61   Carmarthen to Laugharne, period of operation: 16 - 22 October, 1933.
TGR 441/Sp/62   Carmarthen to Laugharne, period of operation: 23 - 29 October, 1933.
TGR 441/Sp/63   Carmarthen to Laugharne, period of operation: 30 Oct - 5 Nov, 1933.

In the meantime, Market Lane garage was renamed 'Pioneer Garage' in January 1934.

The following month, the partnership applied to the Traffic Commissioners for their first short period licence, in order to provide a special excursion.

TGR 457/Sp/1   **Whitland** to **St Davids**. Special excursion on 25/2/1934 only.

Additionally, in view of commencing a tours programme, the following licences to provide a new group of Excursions & Tours were applied for on 21st March, 1934:-

TGR 457/5   **Excursions & Tours** starting from Laugharne.
Objection received from Ebsworth Bros.   *Licence granted 24/10/1934.*

TGR 457/6   **Excursions & Tours** starting from Pendine.
This application was withdrawn on 24/10/1934.

TGR 457/7   **Excursions & Tours** starting from Whitland.
Objections received from Western Welsh Omnibus Co., and GWR (Railway Executive).   *Licence granted 24/10/1934.*

TGR 457/8   **Excursions & Tours** starting from St Clears.
Objections received from Ebsworth Bros., Western Welsh O.C., and GWR (Railway Executive).   *Licence granted 24/10/1934.*

TGR 457/9   **Excursions & Tours** starting from Carmarthen.
Objections received from Ebsworth Bros., Western Welsh O.C., D. Bassett & Sons (Gorseinon) Ltd., and GWR (Railway Executive).
Modifications were added to this application in 9/1934.
Licence granted 24/10/1934.

In retaliation, Williams Bros. objected to Western Welsh's application for Excursions & Tours starting from Carmarthen on 25th April, 1934, and on 21st March, 1934, objected to Daniel Jones & Sons, of Carmarthen, application for Excursions & Tours starting from Carmarthen. They also objected in May 1934, to Ebsworth Bros.' application for Excursions & Tours starting from Carmarthen, and strangely, objected to H.D. Jenkins of Mydrim, application for Excursions & Tours starting from Trelech, with pick-ups at Mydrim.

Above & Below: Guildhall Square, Carmarthen, was the termini of several bus services until 1949, including the services of Tudor Williams Brothers, and Ebsworth Bros. The 1934 Duple bodied Bedford WLB in the foreground is Williams Bros.' TH 4284, which was captured working the Carmarthen – Pendine service. See enlargement below. *(V. Morgan collection).*

Declaration for a Licence and Application for Registration of a HACKNEY CARRIAGE (1) propelled by Steam or Electrically propelled or constructed or adapted to use Coal Gas as fuel or which is not constructed or adapted to use any fuel other than (1) or (2) Otherwise propelled.

(If you have more than six Vehicles OF UNIFORM TYPE group Form R.F. 6)

A.—APPLICATION.

I apply for a licence for the period commencing *1st Jan* and ending *24th March* 193 *34*

VEHICLE being a Hackney Carriage as defined in section four of the Customs and Inland Revenue Act, 1888 :—

Seating capacity (exclusive of driver) see Note (9) overleaf :—

		Annual Licence beginning on 31st December		Annual Licence expiring on 31st December		Amount of Duty
				Other Fuel, Heavy Oil.		
		Full Duty.		Full Duty.		
		£	s.	£	s.	£ s.
Not more than 4 persons	All vehicles	10	0	10	0	
More than 4 but not more than 8 persons	All vehicles	12	0	12	0	
More than 8 but not more than 14 persons {	Fitted entirely with pneumatic tyres	20	0	32	0	
	Other vehicles	30	0	40	0	
More than 14 but not more than 20 persons {	Fitted entirely with pneumatic tyres	30	0	48	0	
	Other vehicles	45	0	60	0	
More than 20 but not more than 26 persons {	Fitted entirely with pneumatic tyres	48	0	65	0	
	Other vehicles	60	0	85	0	13/4/0
More than 26 but not more than 32 persons {	Fitted entirely with pneumatic tyres	57	12	90	0	
	Other vehicles	72	0	110	0	
More than 32 but not more than 40 persons {	Fitted entirely with pneumatic tyres	67	4	108	0	
	Other vehicles	84	0	135	0	
More than 40 but not more than 48 persons {	Fitted entirely with pneumatic tyres	76	16	126	0	
	Other vehicles	98	0	160	0	
More than 48 but not more than 56 persons {	Fitted entirely with pneumatic tyres	86	8	148	0	
	Other vehicles	108	0	195	0	
More than 56 but not more than 64 persons {	Fitted entirely with pneumatic tyres	96	0	170	0	
	Other vehicles	120	0	205	0	
Additional for each person in excess of 64.... {	Fitted entirely with pneumatic tyres	1	10	2	10	
	Other vehicles					

B.—PARTICULARS OF VEHICLE. (For periods other than annual see overleaf.)

(a) Has the vehicle been previously registered under the Roads Act, 1920 ? _____

If not :—

(i) Is it a new vehicle ? _____ *No*
If so, evidence of this such as the Sales Delivery Note, invoice or the like should be supplied _____

(ii) If not a new vehicle a satisfactory explanation must be supplied as to why it has not been previously registered _____

(b) Index Mark and Number (if any) ___ *BX 7236*

(c) Type and colour of body (if alternative bodies are kept for use, particulars and colour of each should be given) *Blue & Cream*

(d) Manu-facturer's
{ Name _____ *W & G W & G* *Bus*
{ Description of Vehicle _____ *Bus*
{ Chassis Type, Letter and No. _____ *3559*
{ Horse power _____

(e) If internal combustion engine give
{ Number of cylinders _____
{ Internal diameter of cylinders _____

(f) Wheel plan (e.g. four wheeler, rigid or articulated six wheeler, etc.) _____

(g) Number of axles to which drive is applied _____

| (h) Weight unladen. | Tons. | Cwt. | Qrs. | Lbs. |
| | 3 | 16 | 2 | - |

(i) Type of Tyres
{ Front _____ *Pneumatic*
{ Middle _____
State whether pneumatic or otherwise { Rear _____ *Pneumatic*

(j) Whether propelled by _____

Steam _____
Electricity _____
Coal Gas _____
Petrol _____ *Petrol*
Heavy Oil _____

(k) Seating capacity (exclusive of driver) See Note 8 overleaf. *26*

(l) Is the body of the vehicle specially constructed to provide space for standing passengers ?

C.—DECLARATION.

I DECLARE THAT I AM A PERSON WHOSE BUSINESS IT IS TO SELL VEHICLES OR LET VEHICLES FOR HIRE AND THAT THE FOREGOING DECLARATION FOR A LICENCE AND APPLICATION FOR REGISTRATION CONTAINS A FULL AND TRUE ACCOUNT OF THE PARTICULARS WHICH THE LAW REQUIRES ME TO STATE, AND THAT THE VEHICLE IS ORDINARILY KEPT BY ME AT _____

[I FURTHER DECLARE THAT THE VEHICLE HAS NOT BEEN OR WILL NOT BE USED BY ME BETWEEN THE DATE OF EXPIRATION OF THE LAST LICENCE AND THE DATE OF COMMENCEMENT OF THE LICENCE FOR WHICH APPLICATION IS NOW MADE.]

The words within the bracket [ ] should be deleted if the vehicle has not previously been licensed, or if the application is for a licence for a period immediately following the period covered by the last licence.

In the case of limited liability companies, the name and address of the registered office of the Company should be given and the Declaration should be signed by the Managing Director or the Secretary. In the case of a private firm, the names by which it is ordinarily known should be given, and the names of the partners, together with the signature of one of the partners. If this Declaration is signed by an agent or steward, the fact must be clearly indicated, and the full name and address of both principal or employer, and that of the agent or steward must be inserted.

Usual Signature ___ *Tudor Williams*

Name in full (IN BLOCK CAPITALS.) *The Garage*

Address _____ *Langland*

Date ___ *Jan 15th* ___ 193 *4* [P.T.O.]

Above: Motor Taxation form for the company's W&G (Willy & George Du-Cros Ltd), **BX 7236**, which the company purchased from the defunct Llanelly Express Co, (Jones Bros., Brynteg, Upper Tumble), in January 1934. *(Courtesy of CTPG).*

26

Above: Two W & G (Willie & George Du-Cros Ltd) buses leaving the factory at Acton Vale, London W3, in 1926, for unidentified South Wales operators. The one on the left is an 'L' type, (Long Wheel Base), which would be identical to **BX 7236** mentioned opposite. Tudor Williams' comment regarding W & G buses was, "they were not a bad bus, and quite fast too, but as time progressed, it was difficult to locate spare parts for them". Manufacture of W & G buses ceased in 1935. W & G had very close links with 'Napier', another vehicle manufacturer from the early days. *(V. Morgan collection).*

It was common knowledge that the Williams family were very influential people in the Township of Laugharne, and had business interests in other fields. They owned several properties and employed many people in the community, who were given a home as part of the job, but alternatively received lower wages.

Interestingly, Tudor Williams was elected Portreeve of the Township in October 1934, a title normally held for one year, but due to his popularity, he was re-elected for a further two years, 1935 and 1936.

Once a Portreeve completes their term in office, they automatically gain the title of Alderman, and attend the fortnightly court meetings of the Corporation, but they have no say in matters of the court. Additionally, they can stand for re-election at the end of a term in office, or upon the death of a Portreeve.

On 20th March, 1935, however, another new stage carriage service licence was applied for:-

TGR 457/10   **Laugharne** to **Whitland**.
             via: St Clears, Bankyfelin, St Clears, and Whitland. (Schooldays only).
             Objections received from Western Welsh, and GWR (Railway Executive),
             on 29/5/1935.   *Licence granted 10/7/1935.*

In retaliation, Williams Bros. once again lodged an objection to Western Welsh's licence renewals for Carmarthen to Narberth, (TGR 441/46), and Narberth Square to Tenby, via Templeton, Kings Moor, and Saundersfoot Road (TGR 441/86). Nevertheless they were granted!

Above: This bulbous looking Thornycroft 'Dainty' DF/FB4/1, **TH 6817**, had C26F coachwork built by R.E.A.L. Carriage Works, Pope's Lane, Ealing, London, W5. It was purchased by the company in March 1936, when the chassis was listed at £350.
Below: Is a rear and offside view of the same Thornycroft 'Dainty', registered **TH 6817**. *(Both views J.I. Thornycroft & Co).*

<u>Above:</u> Another view of the 26 seat Thornycroft 'Dainty', **TH 6817**, which is pictured here on lay-over, with its driver, Theophilus Jones, standing proudly at the front. Theophilus worked with the company for most of his working life.
(Photo courtesy of Winston John, Theo Jones's son-in-law, who also drove for Williams Bros. in the 1960s).

<u>Above:</u> A Western Welsh, Duple bodied Bedford WTB, at Pentre Road, St Clears, in 1938. This view, looking westward along the original A40 trunk road to Pembrokeshire, also takes in the junction with Station Road (B4299 to Mydrim), on the right.

GARDEN FETE

AND

BAZAAR

TO BE HELD AT

COOMB, LLANGUNNOCK

(By kind permission of Lord & Lady Kylsant)

ON

THURSDAY, 10th SEPTEMBER, 1936

To be opened at 2.30 p.m. by
Sir E. MARLAY SAMSON, K.B.E., K.C.

STALLS.—Glass, China, Fancy, Useful Produce, Side Shows.

Decorated Bicycle Competition (Ladies and Gents). Slow Bicycle Race.

TEA: Adults 9d., Children 6d.

Two large marquees provided.

Loud Speaker Van with Music.

AUCTION during Bazaar.

ADMISSION: 6d., Children 3d.

DANCE IN ST. CYNOG'S HALL IN THE EVENING.

Admission: 1/6 including Refreshments.

'Bus Service between Sarnau and Coomb.

ALSO

BUSES

(WILLIAMS BROS.)

WILL LEAVE

GUILDHALL SQUARE, CARMARTHEN

At 2 O'clock.

Return Fare, ONE SHILLING.

(3326—4:9)

Above: This notice appeared in a local newspaper on 4th September, 1936. It appears that Williams Bros. provided transport to the event, but the service was not registered with the Traffic Commissioners in accordance with the Road Traffic Act 1930. The event was on a Thursday – Williams Bros. had a licence to run that route on Saturdays only, and fair days at Carmarthen.

Above: King St., Laugharne in 1938, showing the Brown's Hotel (right) and Brown's Hotel Garage left, which were both purchased by Ebie Williams (Tudor Williams' brother/business partner) in 1937. Brown's Hotel Garage, had been renamed Central Garage by the previous tennants, Ebsworth Bros., who hastily moved to another location when Ebie bought it.

In 1938, the government announced plans to build an 'Inter Service Small Arms Experiment Establishment' at Llanmiloe, near Pendine. It was developed between 1938 and 1940, by the Ministry of Supply, with temporary headquarters at the Beach Hotel in Pendine. Prefabricated bungalows were erected on the compulsory acquired grounds of Llanmiloe House in December 1941, to accommodate a workforce that had transferred from similar establishments at Foulness, and Shoeburyness, in Essex, and from Hythe, in Hampshire.

However, after World War 2 ended, the Ministry of Defence decided that Pendine should become a permanent establishment for the testing and evaluation of a wide variety of other weapons, rather than just focus on 'small arms'.

Renamed the 'Proof & Experimental Establishment' (P & E E), there was further expansion, and by the mid 1950's, 'firing ranges' had been built, and expanded to cover an area of around 7 miles in length, and employed around 2,000 people. Further expansion at the establishment, finally give employment to local people, many of whom were shipped in daily from surrounding towns and villages.

Transport contracts to convey the extra personnel employed at the 'P & E E' were initially awarded to Ebsworth Bros. in 1947, but in due course further routes were added, requiring extra vehicles, which were then contracted to Williams Bros.

Incidentally, the Ministry of Supply had a fleet of Bedford buses based at the Establishment, but they worked mainly internally.

Left: The only photograph I have been able to locate of Williams Bros.' Dennis 'Lancet II', **EPK 134**, is this partial view which was taken at Guildhall Square, Carmarthen. This coach was bodied by Dennis Motors themselves, to C32F layout, becoming a demonstrator for Dennis Motors, Guildford, in January 1937, and passed to Williams Bros. in June 1937. The date of this photograph is thought to be post-war, and the gentleman in view, William Mervyn Roberts, was presumed to be its driver. That theory is now in doubt, as Mervyn worked for Ebsworth Bros. from around 1927, becoming a shareholder and garage manager at Ebsworth Bros., after its incorporation in 1945.

(Courtesy of James & Joan Griffiths).

Lower picture: This view shows a *similar* Dennis 'Lancet' that was bodied by Dennis Motors (EX 9656). It has only been included for readers to visualise how EPK 134 above would have looked with its pleasing lines. It incorporated a stepped waist rail, sloping floor, and a quarter light window incorporated into the near-side of its half-cab coachwork.

(Omnibus Society / The Bus Archive).

World War II commenced on 3rd September, 1939, and within a few days the company were compelled to introduce emergency timetables, in order to conserve fuel when fuel rationing began on 16th September. Services were reduced to a very basic frequency – merely maintaining services to accommodate workers. Licences to operate Excursions & Tours were suspended, in order to conserve fuel and rubber, as were the licences for Express Carriage services three years later. During the war years, licences to provide extra services, or any modification to existing services had to be applied for as usual, but were only authorised by the Ministry of Defence (Ministry of War Transport).

In addition to this, War Department Officials toured all bus and coach operators in Britain, in July 1940, requisitioning buses and coaches for military use, usually taking the operators best buses and coaches. In Williams Bros.' case, nothing was commandeered.

As war progressed, business became relatively quiet in comparison with other operators in Carmarthenshire. There are no records of 'workers services' being sanctioned to Tudor Williams Bros. by the Ministry of War Transport, but one stage carriage service was taken over at an unknown date during the hostilities, from Henry Daniel Jenkins of Ty-newydd Garage, Mydrim, which ran between the village of Mydrim and Carmarthen town, on Wednesdays and Saturdays only (market days and fair days). It was operated with a defence permit during the hostilities, on TGR457/11, and was renewed in March 1947, with the same application number.

Reflecting on the company's tranquillity during the war years, was the fact that no vehicles were acquired during the hostilities, except for a Ford van, BTH 629, which was registered to Tudor Williams' son, Tudor Evelyn Williams, of 'Cottage Farm', Laugharne, and licensed for 'Goods/Agriculture'. Tudor junior, who was also known as 'Tudie', was the only son of Alderman Tudor Williams, founder of the Williams Bros. business. The location of Cottage Farm, however, remains a mystery!

In the meantime, Ebsworth Bros. decided it was time to form a limited company, in order to safeguard themselves from heavy losses in the event of business failure. Ebsworth Brothers Ltd, was incorporated on 22nd August, 1944, as company number 0389376, and the directors were listed as John Lewis Ebsworth and his wife, Lilian Edna Ebsworth, of Clifton House Laugharne. Further details of the incorporation can be found on page 159.

Ebsworth Bros.' operator identification number changed to TGR 3563, in November 1945, due to the change of entity after incorporation, i.e. Ebsworth Brothers Limited.

Above: A fantastic shot of Dennis Griffiths driving the former United Welsh, Albion 'Venturer', **FCY 766.** *(Roy Marshall).*

THE POST WAR YEARS

After the wartime hostilities were over, the company purchased their first double-deck buses, and in September 1946, road service licences which had been under the strict control of the Ministry of War Transport, throughout the war and immediate post-war period, finally reverted back to the Ministry of Transport's Traffic Commissioners' control, thus returning services to normal pre-war working patterns.

As a direct result of all this, a few modifications were made to Williams Bros.' road service licences, when their renewals were applied for in March 1947, as shown below:-

TGR 457/11   **Mydrim** to **Carmarthen (Guildhall Square)**.
via: St Clears, Bankyfelin, and Johnstown.
[1] To run on Wednesdays, Saturdays and fair days at Carmarthen only.
The licence was previously issued to H.D. Jenkins of Mydrim.
Service presently operated under defence permit.
Granted with condition [1] above, 17/9/1947.

TGR 457/2   **Carmarthen (Guildhall Square)** to **Pendine**
via: Bankyfelin, St Clears, and Laugharne.
Condition [1] was altered: The part of the service between Laugharne and Pendine, to be run all year round.
Conditions [2 and 3] remained the same.   *Granted 17/9/1947.*

TGR 457/3   **Carmarthen (Guildhall Square)** to **Llangunnock (Llangynog)**.
via: Johnstown and Sarnau. *To operate on Saturdays and days when Fairs & Marts are held in Carmarthen.*   *Granted 17/9/1947.*

TGR 457/4   **St Clears (Railway Station)** to **Pendine**
via: Laugharne.
The part of the service between Laugharne and Pendine, to be run all year round.   *Granted 17/9/1947.*

It will be noticed that the Excursions &Tours licences TGR 457/5, 7, 8, 9, were not renewed.

On 26th May, 1948, however, Williams Bros. submitted an application to modify the route of TGR 457/11, with respect to extend the service beyond Mydrim, and start it from Trelech. An objection was received from David Jones, 'Ffoshelig', Newchurch, Carmarthen, which resulted in Williams Bros. withdrawing the application on 18th August, 1948.

In retaliation, Williams Bros., in conjunction with Western Welsh, objected to David Jones 'Ffoshelig's application on 23rd July, 1948, to take over H.D. Jenkins, of Mydrim's Wednesday and Saturday only service between Trelech and Carmarthen, via Groesffordd, Pantygroes, Mydrim, Sarnbwrla and Llethrach. David Jones however, received his request.

By 1949, buses were increasing in size, and at the same time, several operators were introducing double-deck vehicles. As a direct result of this, Carmarthenshire County Council officials became concerned about the congestion and safety aspect around Carmarthen's Guildhall Square, with so many bus services terminating there.

The council officials asked the Traffic Commissioners for assistance, and the problem was solved in August 1949, when all services terminating at Guildhall Square, were relocated to other parts of the town. Tudor Williams Brothers and Ebsworth Bros. were relocated to a point in Lammas Street, outside the 'Drovers Arms', some 300 yards away from Guildhall Square. Other operators relocated from Guildhall Square in August 1949, included Davies Brothers, Pencader, with daily services to Llandyssul and Lampeter, Daniel Saunders Davies, New Inn, with a market days only service, newly inherited from David Edgar Jones, of Pencader, and the market days only services of Daniel Davies, Felingwm, and Henry Isaac Lewis, Llanfynydd.

Above: Pictured here at Lammas Street, Carmarthen, working the Wednesday & Saturday only, Mydrim to Carmarthen service, is **EWO 583**, a 1943 Bedford OWB, with 'utility' style Duple body. This bus had been somewhat modernised, with side panel trim, wheel nut guards (chrome hub caps), sliding windows, and re-seated from 32 to 28, with the fitment of new 'Dunlopillo' seating. **EWO 583** had been acquired in November 1947, from Ralph's Garages Ltd, of Abertillery, Monmouthshire, (f/n 83), a member of the large Red & White group, and was scrapped in November 1963. Incidentally, Lammas Street became the termini for Williams Bros. and Ebsworth Bros.' services in 1949, when the local authority banned the use of Guildhall Square as a termini. *(Roy Marshall).*

Right: Williams Bros. bought this former Sheffield Corpn. (262), 1934 AEC Regent 0661, **AWB 62**, with Park Royal L27/26R bodywork, from the dealer Stanley J. Davies of Penygraig, Glamorganshire, in June 1948. There has been a lot of controversy whether this vehicle was operated, but I can confirm that it *was* operated by Williams Bros. It arrived at Laugharne, fitted with an 8.8 litre petrol engine, but was retrofitted with an 8.8 litre, oil engine by June 1955.

(Alan B. Cross).

Below: A second former Sheffield C.T. AEC Regent 0661 with petrol engine, arrived at Laugharne from the same source in June 1948. Although, this particular one, **CWA 490**, dated from May 1936, and carried Weymann H30/26R bodywork. This was licenced in August 1948, and is pictured here at Lammas Street, Carmarthen, accompanied by Williams Bros.' Dennis Lancet II, DWW 492. The Lancet was new as a box van with Ripponden & District in 1939, but was re-bodied with this Willowbrook DP39F body in June 1942, for Hurst, of Longton, Staffordshire. Williams Bros. purchased that from Davies Bros. Pencader (27), in December 1950, still fitted with a petrol engine.

(D.A. Jones).

37

Above: This view of Williams Bros' Dennis 'Lance III', **ETH 204**, displays its original livery layout, outside the Drovers Arms, in Carmarthen. The Singer 10 in the backdrop is registered TH 3850, and propped up against the Drovers Arms wall, is Williams Brothers' timetable, a blackboard with the times crudely handwritten in chalk (see page 58). *(V. Morgan collection).*

Above: **ETH 204** is pictured here at the Pendine terminus of the jointly operated Carmarthen - Pendine service, the forecourt of the Springwell Inn, where the conductor acted as a 'banksman' for the reverse manuver. *(V. Morgan collection).*

Above and Below: ETH 204 was painted red, white and blue for the Coronation of Queen Elizabeth II, in 1953, and was the only double decker acquired 'new' by the company. It was bodied by D.J. Davies of Merthyr, at their Treforest coachbuilding activities, and was identical to the 'Lance' supplied to Ebsworth Bros. six months later, which had consecutive chassis numbers. Tudor Williams stated that the bodywork on this vehicle was 'terrible'.　　　　(**Above**: *J.S. Cockshot.* **Below**: *Peter Yeomans).*

Above: This 1936 AEC Regal, **CVT 676**, with Willowbrook DP39F bodywork (later DP37F), arrived in March 1949, from Stoke Motors, Stoke-on-Trent, and is pictured in Market Lane, Laugharne, alongside Williams Bros.' 'Engine House'. This engine house generated and supplied the only electricity available for the town, from late 1920s until mid-1950s. *(Alan B. Cross)*.

Above: Another view of **CVT 676**, the Willowbrook bodied AEC Regal, acquired from Stoke Motors. *(John Bennett collection)*.

As mentioned earlier, Ebsworth Bros. received all of the workers service contracts to the Proof & Experimental Establishment, at Llanmilo (Pendine) in 1947, but due to further expansion at the Establishment in 1949, Williams Bros. received a share of the work too.

On 31st August, 1949, Williams Bros. and Ebsworth Bros. applied individually for a 'new' jointly operated workmen's stage carriage service licence:-

Williams Bros.' application read as follows:-

TGR 457/12   **Carmarthen** to **Pendine (P & E E, Llanmilo)**
via: Bankyfelin, St Clears, and Laugharne. *(Mon to Sat).*
Assisted Travel Scheme, 3/- weekly deducted from wages at source.
Granted 21/12/1949, with special condition: The vehicles used on this authorised service are to be garaged in Carmarthen from Mondays to Fridays inclusive each week, during which the service is to be operated.

It has been mentioned earlier in the story about the Williams family's generosity, but the arrangement of giving employees a home as part of the job, in exchange for lower wages, got the Williamses into deep trouble in June 1950. The commotion eventually involved the South Wales area Traffic Commissioners, who posted the following notice in Notices & Proceedings dated 13th September, 1950:-

'Under powers derived from Section 74 of the Road Traffic Act, 1930, the Licensing Authority for Public Service Vehicles for the South Wales Traffic Area, propose to hold a Public Sitting, to afford Messrs Tudor Williams Bros., of Pioneer Garage, Laugharne, Carmarthen, an opportunity to show cause why the road service licences held by them and scheduled below, should not be revoked or suspended for wilful breach of the condition attached to the licences, it having been decided by the Industrial Court sitting at Cardiff, on the 16th June, 1950, that the rate of wages, and conditions of employment by them, in connection with the operation of public service vehicles, and the conditions of their employment, are less favourable than the wages which would be payable, and the conditions which would have to be observed under a contract which complied with the requirement of a resolution of the House of Commons for the time being in force applicable to contracts with Government Departments'.

Schedule

Licence No.	Stage Carriage Service.	Ref. No.
G. 03074	Pendine - Carmarthen	TGR 457/2
G. 03001	Llangunnock - Carmarthen	TGR 457/3
G. 03002	St Clears - Laugharne - Pendine	TGR 457/4
G. 03003	Mydrim - Carmarthen	TGR 457/11
G. 01129	Carmarthen - Pendine (P&EE)	TGR 457/12

'If any person or persons desire to object to this proposal, or make representations concerning it, he or they shall, within seven days from the date of this notice, give notice in writing to the Licensing Authority (and in the case of any person other than the holders of the road service licences, to the holders) of his or their objection and/or representation and of the specific ground on which they are based'.

'Notice of the time, date, and venue of the Public Sitting will be published in Part II of a future issue of Notices & Proceedings'.

Four weeks later, on 11th October, 1950, the above notice was cancelled. An amicable arrangement had been agreed with the employees involved!

As a direct result of this, Williams Brothers *and* Ebsworth Brothers asked the Traffic Commissioners for permission to revise fares on their shared Carmarthen to Pendine service.

The proposed fare table, dated 3rd January, 1951, is reproduced below:-

```
Carmarthen.
2d.    Johnstown.
4d.    3d.    Travellers' Rest.
5d.    4d.    3d.    Maesyprior.
6d.    5d.    4d.    3d.    Pass Bye.
8d.    6d.    5d.    4d.    3d.    Sarnau Road.
9d.    7d.    6d.    5d.    4d.    3d.    Bankyfelin.
10d.   8d.    7d.    6d.    5d.    4d.    3d.    Rushmoor.
11d.   9d.    8d.    7d.    6d.    5d.    4d.    3d.    New Church.
1/1    11d.   10d.   9d.    8d.    7d.    6d.    5d.    3d.    Upper St. Clears.
1/3    1/1    1/-    11d.   10d.   8d.    7d.    6d.    5d.    3d.    Lower St. Clears.
1/4    1/2    1/1    1/-    11d.   9d.    8d.    7d.    6d.    5d.    3d.    Morfa Bach.
1/5    1/3    1/2    1/1    1/-    10d.   9d.    8d.    7d.    6d.    5d.    3d.    Cross Inn.
1/7    1/5    1/4    1/3    1/2    1/-    11d.   10d.   9d.    8d.    7d.    5d.    3d.    Laugharne.
1/9    1/7    1/6    1/5    1/4    1/2    1/1    1/-    11d.   9d.    8d.    7d.    6d.    Mansion.
1/11   1/9    1/8    1/7    1/6    1/4    1/3    1/2    1/1    11d.   9d.    8d.    7d.    Plashett.
2/1    1/11   1/10   1/9    1/8    1/6    1/5    1/4    1/3    1/1    11d.   10d.   9d.    Brook.
2/2    2/1    1/11   1/10   1/9    1/7    1/6    1/5    1/4    1/2    1/-    11d.   10d.   Llanmiloe.
2/3    2/2    2/1    2/-    1/11   1/9    1/8    1/7    1/6    1/4    1/2    1/1    1/-    Pendine.
```

```
Laugharne.
4d.    Mansion.
5d.    3d.    Plashett.
6d.    4d.    3d.    Brook.
8d.    6d.    5d.    4d.    Llanmiloe.
9d.    8d.    7d.    6d.    3d.    Pendine.

Special Return : Laugharne—Pendine  ..  1/3.

Children over 3 and under 14 years of age, half-fare, with
    minimum fare of 1d.
```

		Ordinary Returns :—	
S.	R.	S.	R.
4d. ..	7d.	1/4 ..	2/3
5d. ..	9d.	1/5 ..	2/5
6d. ..	10d.	1/7 ..	2/8
7d. ..	1/-	1/9 ..	3/-
8d. ..	1/3	1/11 ..	3/2
9d. ..	1/5	2/1 ..	3/5
11d. ..	1/7	2/2 ..	3/6
1/1 ..	1/9	2/3 ..	3/8
1/3 ..	2/-	2/6 ..	4/-

This fare table was withdrawn six weeks later, and substituted with a revised fare table, asking for an increase of 25%, which was granted to both operators on 23rd May, 1951.

Returning to August 1950, Ebsworth Bros. asked for the special condition applied to their jointly operated workers express carriage service TGR 3563/10, regarding garaging a vehicle overnight at Carmarthen, to be deleted from the licence. Their request was granted on 22nd November, 1950.

Above: Tudor Williams Brothers had a penchant for the Dennis marque, and purchased this second-hand Dennis 'Lancet III', with D.J. Davies 35 seat coachwork, from E.R. Forse of Cardiff, in December 1949. *(Peter Yeomans).*

Above: This petrol engine Dennis 'Lancet II', **DWW 492**, has a very interesting history. It was new as a van in December 1939, to Ripponden & District, but was re-bodied in June 1942, with this Willowbrook DP39F body, for Hurst, Longton, Staffs. It later passed to Hackett, Hazel Grove, Stockport, and to Davies Bros., Pencader (27), in August 1948. Williams Bros. acquired it from Davies Bros. in December 1950, and operated it until January 1960, by such time it had been fitted with a diesel engine. It's pictured here at Lammas Street, Carmarthen, circa 1952. *(D.A. Jones).*

43

Following suit 12 months later, Williams Bros. asked the Traffic Commissioners for the same modification on their licence TGR 457/12, to be 'in-line' with the modification granted to joint operator, Ebsworth Bros. This was to remove the special condition of garaging at Carmarthen, the vehicle used on the jointly operated workers service, Carmarthen to Pendine (P & E E, Llanmilo). Their request was granted six weeks later on 9th January, 1952.

In March 1952, Williams Bros. applied jointly with Ebsworth Bros. for permission to modify licences TGR 457/2, 3, 4 & 11 and TGR 3563/1 & 2 respectively as follows:-,

[1] To introduce revised weekly and season tickets, as authorised to Western Welsh O.C., and other companies.

[2] To charge a booking fee of 6d on interchangeable tickets.

Condition [1] was granted to both parties, and condition [2] was refused to both parties, on 28th May, 1952.

Above: By 1951, Tudor Williams Bros. and Ebsworth Bros. had settled their differences, and became good friends. Ebsworth Bros. assisted Williams Bros. with their engineering problems, and sent fitters over to help them with maintenance issues. However, by August 1951, Tudor Williams Bros. had bought this 1930 Leyland 'Titan' TD1, **GJ 7537**, with a 1935 Burlingham H29/26R body off Ebsworth Bros. Interestingly, it had received a second-hand radiator from a Leyland TS1 'Tiger' sometime during its working life, as seen in this view, after sale to Lansdowne Luxury Coaches, Leytonstone, London E11, in 1955, still carrying Williams Bros.' livery. *(The Bus Archive).*

Above: This AEC Regent, **RD 5361**, with Park Royal lowbridge bodywork, is pictured at 'The Grist' in Laugharne, en route for Pendine in 1954. It was new to Reading Corporation Transport (10), in September 1935, and retrofitted with a diesel engine by them in 1946/7. It arrived at Laugharne in March 1954, via Beech's Garage (dealer), Hanley, Staffs. The building in the backdrop has since been converted into the local 'Spar' shop, with flats above. *(Roy Marshall).*

Right: A splendid front and near side view of the Park Royal L26/25R bodied AEC Regent, **RD 5361**. This view was taken on the bus stand, outside the 'Drovers Arms', Lammas Street, Carmarthen, as it worked the Carmarthen to Pendine service. The West End Café is just visible in the background – a famous refreshment room for bus crews and passengers alike. Just visible behind the bus, is a rare 1950 Singer 'Hunter' SM1500 registered JUY 389. Not many of that marque have survived into preservation.
(V. Morgan collection).

In 1954, Ebsworth Brothers Ltd., found themselves in serious financial difficulty, and could not pay their hire purchase. Their financier, Julian Hodge of Cardiff, who was also a director at Ebsworth Bros., wanted his money, so he offered the business to a former work colleague at the GWR, T.G. Davies, who was the General Manager of Western Welsh. The offer was accepted and Western Welsh took over the business on 6ᵗʰ December 1954. The joint service arrangement between Williams Bros. and Ebsworth Bros. continued with Western Welsh.

Above: This vehicle is not what it appears to be. **EWM 347** was a Daimler CWA6, with utility style Northern Counties H30/26R body, new to Southport Corporation (59), in 6/1944. It had been modernised with Dunlopillo (soft) seating by 1947, long before Williams Bros. acquired it from AMCC (dealer) in April 1955. By July 1958, Williams Bros. had fitted it with an AEC 8.8 litre engine and radiator, salvaged from withdrawn AEC Regent, JX 2301.   *(R. Marshall).*

Left: There's been quite a lot of controversy as to when **EWM 347** received its AEC radiator. This photograph of **EWM 347**, with the Beach Hotel, Pendine, in the backdrop, was quite an early attempt of mine at bus photography, which I took in July 1958.   *(V. Morgan).*

Above: My first encounter of a Williams Bros. (Pioneer) bus was a ride on this particular vehicle, in the upper deck front off-side seat, from Carmarthen to Pendine, for a 7 day camping holiday, in July 1958. This AEC Regent, **FWL 644**, with Park Royal H28/24R bodywork, was new to City of Oxford MS (K119) in 3/1938, and was acquired by Williams Bros. in May 1955, from Northern General (1400), via AMCC (dealer). *(Roy Marshall).*

Above: This second view of **FWL 644**, was probably taken at the same time as the upper view, as it poses nicely for the camera, on exactly the same spot near the Drovers Arms, in Lammas Street, with the same Austin 10 parked behind it. Just visible in the backdrop is Williams Bros.' Bedford OWB, EWO 583, working the Carmarthen – Mydrim service. *(Roy Marshall).*

Above: Williams Bros. bought **GAW 679**, this fully fronted Burlingham FC35F bodied, Leyland PS1/1 'Tiger', from Lansdowne, London E11, in September 1955. It was new to Whittle, Highley, Salop, in 4/1950, and is pictured here outside W.G. Harvey's paint & wallpaper shop, Lammas St., Carmarthen, accompanied by D. Jones (Ffoshelig) Bedford OB, DTH 999. *(R. Marshall).*

Above: The chassis of this Dennis 'Lancet II' was new to Glenton Tours of London in 1936, and was registered CYU 917. D.J. Davies, Merthyr acquired this in 1945 for their Wheatsheaf Motors' fleet, rebodying it themselves, and re-registering it **HB 5989** in July 1945. Williams Bros. purchased it from Wheatsheaf in November 1956, and ran it for only 2 years. *(Roy Marshall).*

Above: When West Wales Motors, at Tycroes, modernised their fleet in 1958, Williams Bros. purchased their surplus 1946 Albion CX13 'Valkyrie' **CBX 960**. It had been rebodied in April 1951, with this Duple B35F body, and saw a further six years service at Laugharne. More information and the complete history of West Wales Motors can be found in my publication 'Rees & Williams Ltd., and West Wales Motors Ltd'., available at: vernonmorgan.com *(V. Morgan collection).*

Above: One of the most popular buses of its type was the Bedford OB. A total of 12,766 were produced between 1939 and 1951. However, the forward control model, usually a chassis conversion by G.E. Neville & Son, Mansfield, were made in limited numbers, and mostly bodied by Plaxton. Williams Bros. purchased this forward control Bedford OB, **FAB 463**, with Plaxton FC30F coachwork, from Everton, Droitwich in June 1958. It was new to Ward of Bromsgrove in October 1946. *(Roy Marshall).*

Above: This Dennis 'Lancet III', **MPE 410**, with Reading coachwork built to DP35F configuration, was new in July 1948, to Safeguard Coaches, Guildford, Surrey. This one was acquired in October 1958, and withdrawn in June 1967. *(Peter Yeomans).*

Above: A later view of **MPE 410**, taken alongside the garage in Market Lane, which was originally the Mews. *(Roy Marshall).*

Above: A superb view of Lammas St., Carmarthen, showing a range of classic vehicles, including the 1943 Guy Arab I (5LW) with Northern Counties L27/28R body, masquerading as **GHN 385**. This bus was actually GHN 384, the registration plates and chassis plates, were interchanged by the dealer before delivery to Williams Bros. in April 1959. The original GHN 385 was then broken up. This particular vehicle was withdrawn in July 1963, and sold for scrap to Jones, a Cardiff breaker. *(J.S. Cockshot).*

Above: This 1949, Burlingham bodied Dennis 'Lancet III', **HWY 956**, came from Longstaff, Mirfield, West Yorks, in Jan. 1960.

Above: YMF 82 was an AEC Regal IV, with Roe B44F bodywork, which was new in December 1952 as a demonstrator for AEC Ltd, of Southall, Middlesex. It afterwards passed to McGill, of Barrhead, East Renfrewshire, and found its way to Williams Bros. (Pioneer) Laugharne, in June 1959, becoming their first underfloor engine vehicle. *(Peter Yeomans).*

Above: The former AEC demonstrator, **YMF 82**, is seen here on the short promenade at Pendine, departing for Carmarthen via Laugharne. This bus gave the company 10 years service before disposal to V.J. Peters, Pembrey, for further use.

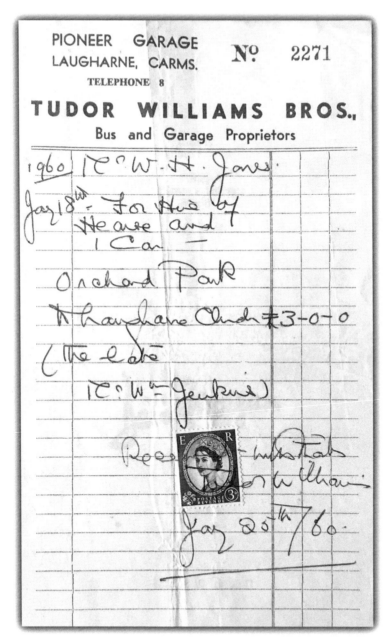

Above: A receipt for the hire of Williams Bros.' hearse and one car, in January 1960. *(Peter Jenkins' collection).*

PIONEER BUSES DAILY TIME-TABLE.

		WEEKDAYS							F	SUNDAYS		
		a.m.	a.m.	p.m.	p.m.	p.m.	p.m.	p.m.	p.m.	p.m.	p.m.	p.m.
Pendine	dep.	✱ 8.45	11.0	1. 0	3. 0	5.15	7. 0	9. 0	11.0	4. 0	–	8. 0
Laugharne	"	9. 0	11.15	1.15	3.15	5.30	7.15	9.15	11.15	4.15	–	8.15
St. Clears	"	9.15	11.25	1.25	3.25	5.40	7.25	9.25		4.20	–	8.20
Bankyfelin	"	9.25	11.35	1.35	3.35	5.50	7.35	9.35		4.25	–	8.25
Carmarthen	arr.	9.45	11.55	1.55	3.55	6.10	7.55	9.55		4.40	6.45	8.40
								X		–	6.55	8.55

		a.m.	noon	p.m.	p.m.	p.m.	p.m.	p.m.		p.m.	p.m.	p.m.
Carmarthen	dep.	10. 0	12.0	2. 0	4.15	6. 0	8. 0	10. 0		3. 0	7. 0	9. 0
Bankyfelin	"	10.20	12.20	2.20	4.35	6.20	8.20	10.20		3.15	7.15	9.15
St. Clears	"	10.30	12.30	2.30	4.45	6.30	8.30	10.30		3.30	7.30	–
Laugharne	"	10.40	12.40	2.40	4.55	6.40	8.40	10.40		3.38	7.38	–
Pendine	arr.	10.55	12.55	2.55	5.10	6.55	8.55	–		3.44	7.44	–
										3.55	7.55	–

✱ Denotes Saturdays only: Mondays to Fridays (inclusive) will
start from Laugharne at 9.0a.m.

X Journey to be extended to Pendine on Fridays only.

F Fridays only.

Above: Williams Bros. (Pioneer Buses) timetable, for the Carmarthen - Pendine service, dated 27/10/1963. *(The Bus Archive).*

On 17th February, 1960, Williams Bros. applied for the following three 'Workmen's Express Carriage' service licences:-

TGR 457/13   **Llanddowror** to **Llanmilo (Proof & Experimental Establishment).** via: Red Roses, Amroth, and Pendine. *Monday to Friday.*

TGR 457/14   **Whitland** to **Llanmilo (Proof & Experimental Establishment).** via: Red Roses. *Monday to Friday.*

TGR 457/15   **Summerhill** to **Llanmilo (Proof & Experimental Establishment).** via: Amroth. *Monday to Friday.*

All three applications were granted on 13th April, 1960, with the following conditions:-

Vehicles will be paid for on a mileage basis by the Ministry of Aviation, Government Buildings, Gabalfa, Cardiff. The employees will contribute towards the cost of their conveyance, in accordance with a Travel Assistance Scheme.

It must be noted that Tudor Williams Brothers had for some considerable time, operated these three services unlicensed. The services were known to be operating *before* July 1958.

<u>Above:</u> Partner of the Williams Bros. business, William Fleming Williams (Billie), became the Portreeve of Laugharne Township, in October 1959, and held that position for two consecutive years. After his two year period as Portreeve, he automatically received the title of 'Alderman' in October 1961. An Alderman is simply a past Portreeve. William sadly passed away in December 1969, aged 71. *(Peter Jenkins' collection).*

Above: This Bedford SB1 with Duple 'Midland' B42F bodywork, **UAX 639**, was new to Peake, Pontypool, in 11/1958, but was acquired via Thomas Bros. Llangadog, in June 1961. It's seen here passing the Lark Inn, at 32 Blue Street, Carmarthen. The Lark Inn, had an interesting background, as it was the operating centre of William Petter, an early Carmarthen bus operator, who ran a bus service between Carmarthen and Llandeilo, trading as Lark Motors / Lark Bus Service. Oscar Chess' car showroom next door, had a dealership for 'Rootes Group' cars, Hillman, Humber, Singer, and Sunbeam. *(V. Morgan collection).*

Above: **UAX 639**, pictured at the Carmarthen terminus of the period, Lammas Street, in August 1972.   *(John Bennett).*

Above: The last Dennis 'Lancet' acquired by the Williams family, was **KOE 794**, which is pictured here inside the King Street garage. The coachwork was built by Santus of Wigan, to FC33F layout (later FC35F), and was new to L.E. Bowen, Birmingham, in March 1950 (see below). It had a few owners before arriving at Laugharne in September 1961, from Lords Coaches of Rushden, Northants, and was withdrawn from service in October 1964, but was still inside the King Street garage a year later. **Below:** Is another photograph of **KOE 794**, when it was new to L.F. Bowen, Cotterills Lane, Birmingham. *(V. Morgan collection).*

Above: Tudor Williams & Brothers did not invest much money on timetables. This particular timetable was a fixture in the window of the Drovers Arms, Lammas Street, Carmarthen, which was the departure point of their services. *(The Bus Archive).*

Above: This former United Welsh Services (966), **FCY 766**, 1948 Albion 'Venturer' CX19, with Metro-Cammell H30/26R bodywork, was acquired in January 1962. It is pictured here trundling through the Carmarthenshire countryside between St Clears and Laugharne, as it returned home from Carmarthen with a full load of passengers on a market day. *(Roy Marshall)*.

Below: FCY 766 is pictured here on an off-peak journey near Bancyfelin, heading into Carmarthen. *(V. Morgan collection)*.

On 4th July, 1962, the company applied for the following 'Workmen's Express Carriage' service licence:-

TGR 457/16   **Tenby** to **Llanmilo (Proof & Experimental Establishment).**
via: Tenby (Five Arches), Saundersfoot (main bus stop), Ridgeway, Saundersfoot (Fountain Head), Begelly Cross, Kilgetty Station, Stepaside, Beef's Park Farm, and Marros Church.   *Monday to Friday only.*
Only persons employed at the Proof & Experimental Establishment at Pendine to be carried on this service.
Fares will be subsidised by the Travel Assistance Scheme.

It was granted on 26th September, 1962, superseding an earlier 'Workers Express Carriage' licence, TGR 457/15, for Summerhill to Llanmilo (P & E.E.), which in turn, was surrendered on 26th September, 1962.

The 'Workers Stage Carriage Service' licence, TGR 457/12, between Carmarthen and Pendine (Proof & Experimental Establishment), was withdrawn on 23rd September, 1964.

EAX 645, was a Guy 'Arab' Mk I with 6LW engine, and is seen **above,** leaving King Street garage, and **below**, at Carmarthen. It was new in June 1942, to Red & White Motor Services (L242), with utility type body, and was re-bodied to L27/28RD layout in August 1951, by Brislington Body Works, an associate of the Red & White Group. The gentleman on the left is Tommy Rawles, handyman and bus cleaner, and on the right is Stanley Ormond, transport manager / depot foreman. Stanley previously ran his own bus company in Saundersfoot, which passed to Greens Motors, Haverfordwest in 1932. *(V. Morgan collection).*

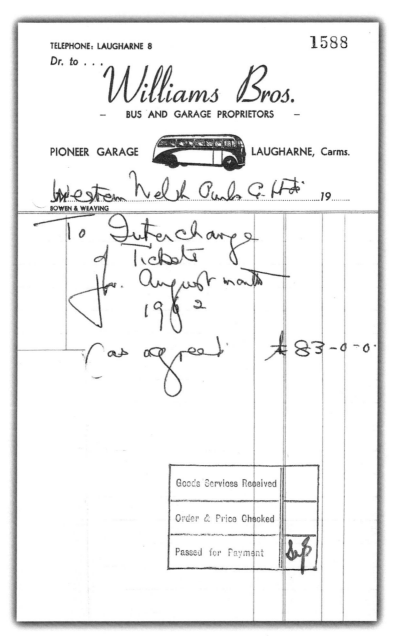

Above: Ths invoice to the Western Welsh Omnibus Co., dated August 1962, was billing Western Welsh for acceptance of their return tickets, under the interavailability agreement for that particular month. *(CTPG Archive).*

Above: A rear end view of Guy Arab, **EAX 645**, inside King Street garage, shows how the Williams Brothers utilised every available panel on their buses for advertising – an additional source of revenue for the business. *(R.F. Mack).*

Above: The ubiquitous Bedford OB, **UMP 532**, with Duple 'Vista' C29F coachwork. There were 12,766 Bedford OBs produced between 1939 and 1951, and not many British bus operators of the early post war period can say they never had one. Williams Bros. bought this from Gwynne Price, Trimsaran, in September 1963. It is seen here at Lammas Street, Carmarthen, upon arrival from Llangynog, with 'Tudie' behind the wheel, using it 'illegally', without a lifeguard rail fitted to the off-side. *(R. Marshall).*

Above & Below: DTH 15, was a 1947 Albion 'Valkyrie' with Duple 'A' 35 seat coachwork, acquired from West Wales Motors, Tycroes (40), in December 1963, having been rebuilt to full-front layout by Thurgood of Ware, in June 1959. Above: it's seen inside Market Lane garage, and below, inside King Street garage. It was withdrawn in February 1968. (Both views R. Marshall).

Above: This Sentinel STC6, registered **YRF 734,** had B44F bodywork built by Sentinel. It was new to Whieldon, Rugeley, Staffs (45), in April 1953, and arrived at Laugharne, in April 1965, via Lewis, Falmouth. It is seen here parked up outside Dylan Thomas' favourite watering hole, Brown's Hotel, owned by Williams Bros. partner, Ebie Williams. Ebie sadly passed away in 1965. This bus left the fleet after a very short while, and was sold to Dolan (Shamrock), Newport, in July 1966.   *(R.F. Mack).*

Above: The first Bristol in the Williams Bros. fleet was this Bristol LS5G, **UEV 829,** in July 1965. It's captured here at St Clears, making a left turn from Pentre Road into High Street, on a journey from Carmarthen to Pendine.   *(V. Morgan collection).*

Above: Williams Bros.' UEV 829 was a Bristol LS5G, with 5 cylinder Gardner engine and ECW (Eastern Coach Works) B43F bodywork. It was new in December 1952, to Eastern National Omnibus Co. (4174), and was built to dual purpose specification with 41 seats and dual entrance. Later rebuilt to B43F layout, and renumbered 1200, it passed to Williams Bros. in July 1965. After 6 years use, it was sold to a dealer near Ludlow in June 1971, for scrap. This August 1968 view, takes in the 'Spring Well' public house, another famous Pendine watering hole, situated at the end of the promenade – and the animal crossing the forecourt is not a pig. The Spring Well forecourt provided a terminus for the services of Williams Bros. Ebsworth Bros. and later Western Welsh, but modern day services, continue up the steep Pendine Hill (B4314), to St. Margaret's Church, were a reverse manoeuvre is carried out, thus serving the upper reaches of Pendine village. Since the demise of Pioneer Buses in 1980, Pendine has been served by several operators. Jones of Login, near Whitland, South Wales Transport, First Cymru Buses, Ffoshelig Coaches of Carmarthen, and is currently served by Taf Valley Coaches of Whitland. *(Courtesy of John Bennett).*

On 29th December, 1965, due to lack of support, the licence for the company's 'pioneering service', TGR 457/4, from St Clears Railway Station to Pendine, was surrendered.

Above: FMO 16 was a Bristol L6B with an ECW B35R body, and was new to Thames Valley Traction Co, in May 1950. It was one of a batch of Bristol 'L's transferred to United Welsh Services, Swansea (f/n 541), in March 1960, and was purchased by Williams Bros. in February 1966, giving them excellent service until 1973. *(Alan Broughall).*

Above: Another view of the Bristol L6B, **FMO 16**, pictured in St Martins Church car park, Laugharne. This location became a regular parking place for Williams Bros.' buses in the 1970s, due to fleet expansion. *(V. Morgan collection).*

Above: This former Thames Valley (557), Bristol LL6B, **FMO 939**, with Eastern Coach Works B39R body, was another vehicle acquired from United Welsh, in December 1965. This view was taken inside Market Lane garage in August 1968, with Tudor's favourite bus, Bedford OB, BVV 418, just visible, along with Ford V8, CYV 207, which once operated as a taxi. *(John Bennett).*

Above: This Guy 'Arab' UF, **SFC 501**, with a Gardner 6HLW engine, was new to South Midland Motor Services (86), in April 1953. Its Leyland style body was built to C41C configuration, by Lydney Coachworks, finished by Brislington Body Works (BBW), all associate companies of South Midland. In July 1960, it was transferred to another associate company, Red & White Motor Services, as UC1552, and renumbered DS1552 in May 1962, passing to Williams Bros. (Pioneer) in July 1966. It is pictured here working an outing to Aberavon Beach, Port Talbot, in 1966. *(Roy Marshall).*

Above: A second view of the former South Midland Motor Services, centre entrance, Guy 'Arab' UF, **SFC 501**, which was part exchanged for a Duple bodied Ford 570E at Vincent Greenhous, the dealers, Hereford, in 1972. *(V. Morgan collection).*

Above: Tudor Williams' favourite bus, **BVV 418**, a 1950 Bedford OB, with Duple 'Vista' C29F coachwork. It was photographed on 4th September, 1971, at Lammas Street, Carmarthen - departure point for the Mydrim service which it was operating. This vehicle was purchased from Owen, Berriew, Montgomeryshire in May 1967. Withdrawn in 1975 and stored until March 1980.

Above: **JWO 221** was a former Red & White Motor Services (U651), 1952 Leyland 'Royal Tiger', fitted with Lydney bodywork finished by BBW to B45F layout. It was acquired in April 1967, and is seen here at King Street, Laugharne with Brown's Hotel and the nearby 'New Three Mariner's' public house in the backdrop. Williams Bros.' Pioneer Garage, was located at the point where the photographer stood to take this view. *(Roy Marshall).*

Left: Another former Red & White Motor Services Leyland 'Royal Tiger' arrived in June 1967, but the C41F bodywork of this one was built entirely by Lydney Coachworks. This was registered **JWO 126**, and is seen here at the company's King Street garage, about to depart on a workers stage carriage service, from the Ministry of Supply's Experimental Establishment at nearby Llanmilo, in August 1968. It was withdrawn from service in June 1973.
(John Bennett).

Above: Another view of the former Red & White (U651), Leyland 'Royal Tiger' PSU1/13, **JWO 221**, taken inside the King Street garage on a day of rest, with sister vehicle JWO 126 parked immediately behind it.   *(Alan Broughall).*

Above: This front off-side view of **JWO 126**, the Lydney bodied Leyland 'Royal Tiger' PSU1/13, was taken when the vehicle was between duties, parked up near the garage in King Street, Laugharne.   *(Alan Broughall).*

January 1968 saw the Transport Minister announce details of the Road Traffic Act 1968, which gave stage carriage bus operators, financial grants of 25% towards the purchase of new service buses, provided they complied with certain requirements of the Ministry of Transport. The intention of the grant scheme was to encourage operators to modernise their fleets and to make buses more competitive with private cars, and in 1970, when the grant was increased to 50%, the rules were extended to include coaches, provided they were used to a sufficient extent on such bus services, and their coach bodies were built with essential modifications that complied to the bus grant specification. The conditions stipulated that operators would have to refund the grant if they sold the vehicle or ceased to use it for stage carriage service within five years of its delivery.

The scheme commenced on 1st September, 1968, and ended in March 1984, but Tudor Williams and his partners, did not take up the offer, and continued to buy pre-used vehicles.

In addition to the bus grant, provision was made to increase the fuel duty rebate, which had been introduced in 1965, from 50% to 100%, (10d to 1/7d a gallon), paid to operators of rural bus services from 1st January, 1969, together with 'Rural Bus Grants' to subsidise uneconomical rural bus services. (Further details of this on page 76).

By December 1968, a change of entity was recorded on the operator licence, due to the death of partner Ebie Fleming Williams in December 1965. Tudor's son, Tudor ('Tudie') who also worked in the business, replaced Ebie on the licence. The new entity read as follows:-

Tudor Williams, Brother, & Son (Tudor Williams, William Williams, and Tudor Evelyn Williams) t/a. William Williams sadly passed away in December 1969, aged 71.

Licences TGR 457/2, 3, 11, 13, 14, 16, were re-applied for under the above new title, and granted in May 1969.

<u>Above:</u> GWO 878 was another former Red & White Guy 'Arab III', acquired from West Wales Motors, Tycroes, Ammanford, (55) in August 1969. This view was taken inside the company's King Street garage in October 1970. *(Alan Broughall).*

Above: This Guy 'Arab III', **GWO 878**, with Duple L27/26RD body was pictured here alongside the garage at Market Lane (right), in October 1970. The building on the left was Williams Brothers' 'engine house' – a place where they generated electricity for the town, under the trading name of Laugharne Electric Supply.   *(P. Yeomans).*

Above: The last two 'deckers' operated by Williams Bros. were Guy 'Arab III', **GWO 878** and **HWO 332**. *(V. Morgan collection).*

<u>Above:</u> **YWN 481**, was a Leyland engine Bedford SB8, with Plaxton 'Embassy I', C41F coachwork, acquired from I. Pursey, 'Caerphilly Greys', Caerphilly, in November 1969. This coach was new in March 1961, to Bryn Demery Coaches, Morriston, Swansea. It was withdrawn by Williams Bros. in 1973, and sold to a dealer at Ludlow for export. *(V. Morgan collection).*

<u>Above:</u> Former Sunderland & District (265), **OUP 662**, was a 1954 Leyland 'Tiger Cub' PSUC1/1, with Saunders Roe B44F body. This bus was purchased off Thomas Bros. Llangadog, Carmarthenshire, in March 1971. *(Alan Broughall).*

It was briefly mentioned on page 72, about the provisions made in the Road Traffic Act 1968, for 'Rural Bus Grants' to subsidise uneconomical rural services. However, at a Carmarthenshire County Council meeting in December 1970, councillors discussed the issue, and stated that bus services should not be subsidised from the rates; they should be subsidised with funding from central government, and refused to allow funding to Western Welsh O.C. when they applied for subsidies on several uneconomical services.

In conjunction with driver issues in West Wales, Western Welsh gave the mandatory notice to the Traffic Commissioners, and abandoned *all* services operating in South West Wales. Their Carmarthen depot at St David's Street, and affiliated Laugharne outstation closed on 30th April, 1971.

In the meantime, the Traffic Commissioners invited interested parties to apply for the road service licences previously held by Western Welsh, resulting in a few erroneous entries published in Notices & Proceedings immediately afterwards, which have proven to be incorrect.

In March 1971, the Williams partnership submitted an application to take over all three road service licences operated by Western Welsh, from their Laugharne outstation.

The applications were as follows:-

TGR 457/17 **Laugharne** to **Pendine (MoS, Llanmilo)**. Express Carriage.
via: Broadway, Brook, Llanmilo, and Central Site.
Previous licence granted to Western Welsh (TGR 441/643).

TGR 457/18 **Meidrim** to **Pendine (MoS, Llanmilo)**. Express Carriage.
via: Bancyfelin, St Clears and Laugharne.
Previous licence granted to Western Welsh (TGR 441/645).

At the same time, the company asked for a modification of their Carmarthen to Pendine licence TGR 457/2, in order to incorporate the stage carriage journeys previously authorised to Western Welsh between Carmarthen and Pendine (*TGR 441/640*, route No.411), increasing daily journeys on Mondays to Fridays to 8, Saturdays to 9, Sundays as normal. And an increase in fares was also asked for.

All three applications were granted on 15th September, 1971, and in the meantime, licences for unforeseen services were issued to operate the above two Express Carriage services:-

TGR 457/Sp/10 **Laugharne** to **Pendine (MoS)**. Period of operation 2/5/71 to 26/6/71.

TGR 457/Sp/11 **Meidrim** to **Pendine (MoS)**. Period of operation 2/5/71 to 26/6/71.

TGR 457/Sp/12 **Laugharne** to **Pendine (MoS)**. Period of operation 27/6/71 to 7/8/71.

TGR 457/Sp/13 **Meidrim** to **Pendine (MoS)**. Period of operation 27/6/71 to 7/8/71.

A few months later, another Express Carriage licence for unforeseen service was issued:-
TGR 457/Sp/14 **Laugharne** to **Red Roses**. Period of operation 20/9/71 to 14/11/71.
When all RSL's were renewed in April 1972, a modification was made to TGR 457/3. The Carmarthen to Llangynog service was re-routed to run via Alltycnap Rd, instead of Sarnau.

Right: This view of Tudor Williams (senior) was published in a trade magazine dated July 1971, and read as follows:- 'Highlighting the travel difficulties of senior citizens, it's unlikely to make much impression on the villagers of Laugharne, where the local bus proprietor, Tudor Williams is 80. He's run passengers to the market at Carmarthen every Wednesday and Saturday for 63 years *(Incorrect - Author)*. He started the business back in 1908, with a horse-drawn six-seater wagonette, and when his horses were commandeered in the first world war, he used two Model T saloons, obtaining petrol from the village doctor. Today he's running 12 buses, but the one he favours, is this 1950 Bedford OB 29 seater, BVV 418.' *(V. Morgan collection).*

Below: MUH 157 was a former Western Welsh Leyland 'Tiger Cub' PSUC1/1, with Weymann 'Hermes' B44F body. It was acquired in April 1971 after Western Welsh abandoned all interests in West Wales, due to lack of local authority subsidies, and driver issues – refusing to accept one-man-operation. This view was taken at Pentlepoir, Pembrokeshire, in August 1971. *(John Bennett).*

Above: MUH 161 was one of two Leyland 'Tiger Cubs' (MUH 157/161), with Weymann 'Hermes' B44F bodywork, purchased from Western Welsh O.C. in April 1971. MUH 161 is seen here at King Street, Laugharne, near the garage.   *(Robert Mack).*

Above: Another view taken at King Street, Laugharne, was this view of **TVO 231**, a former East Midlands, 1956 Leyland 'Tiger Cub' PSUC1/2T, with Willowbrook DP41F body, passing former Yorkshire Traction (439), **NHE 112**, a 1958 Leyland 'Tiger Cub' with a Park Royal B44F body. The Williams partnership had a penchant for the economical 'Tiger Cub', nine were purchased between 1971 and 1974. These two were acquired in June 1971 and July 1972 respectively.   *(Peter Yeomans).*

<u>Above:</u> 'Tiger Cub' **TVO 231**, accompanied by 'Tiger Cub' **MUH 157** and Guy 'Arab' **HWO 332**, inside the depot. *(R.F. Mack).*

<u>Above:</u> **110 ACA** was a Bedford SB5, with Duple 'Midland' B40F body, acquired from Williams, Ponciau, in 1971. *(V. Morgan).*

Above: Former Caerphilly UDC (9), **UTX 9**, had an interesting history. The chassis, built in May 1951, was reconditioned by Leyland Motors before being bodied by Massey Bros, in 1956, passing to Caerphilly in July 1956, where it received a 1956 registration. It arrived at Laugharne via Way (scrap dealer), in April 1972, and was withdrawn in November 1974. *(R.F. Mack).*

Above: The first Ford 'PSV' in the fleet was **662 DAB**, a 'Thames Trader' 570E, with Duple 'Yeoman' C41F coachwork, which arrived from Jones Bros. Malvern Link, in 1971. This view, taken at Wogan Street, Laugharne, in August 1971, shows Market Lane garage just visible on the left, and part of the castle wall is visible on the right. *(John Bennett).*

Above: **NHE 112** was a Leyland 'Tiger Cub' PSUC1/1T, with Park Royal B44F body, and was new to Yorkshire Traction (1105) in January 1958. Later renumbered (439), it passed to Williams Bros. in July 1972, where it worked until August 1977. This view was taken in King Street, Laugharne, on 25th May, 1977. *(V. Morgan).*

Above: This view of the former Yorkshire Traction Leyland 'Tiger Cub', **NHE 112**, was taken at 'The Grist', Laugharne, an area prone to flooding with high tides. The bus is returning to base, after working one of the workers services to the Pendine Experimental Establishment at Llanmilo, near Pendine village. *(V. Morgan collection).*

Above: Pictured here at Lammas Street, Carmarthen, with Angel Motors the 'Simca' dealer in the backdrop, is another former Yorkshire Traction, Leyland 'Tiger Cub' PSUC1/1, registered **SHE 173**, which had Metro-Cammell B45F bodywork, and was acquired in August 1972. On its right is Eynon's of Trimsaran, Alexander bodied 'Tiger Cub' RNN 266. The succinct history of Samuel Eynon & Sons' business has recently been published, and is still available from vernonmorgan.com *(Roy Marshall).*

Above: Another view of Williams Bros.' 1961 Leyland 'Tiger Cub', **SHE 173**, inside their King Street Garage. *(R. Edworthy).*

Above: This view of **475 JHO**, a Plaxton 'Embassy III' bodied Bedford SB5, was taken outside the company's Market Lane garage on 30th July, 1977. The building was originally Tudor Williams' Mews, where the business started from in 1908. After its closure in 1980, the founder's daughter-in-law converted into a pottery shop, and has since become a restaurant, known as 'The Portreeve', owned by Alderman Tudor Williams' great-grandson, Max Howells. See picture on page 116. *(V. Morgan).*

Above: Leyland 'Tiger Cub' PSUC1/2, **PMW 386**, with Harrington DP41F coachwork, was new to 'Silver Star', Porton Down, Wiltshire in 1958. This came to Laugharne in March 1973, via Wilts & Dorset (995), and Hants & Dorset. *(V. Morgan collection).*

Sadly, on Tuesday 18th December, 1973, Tudor Evelyn Williams 'Tudie', the only son of Alderman Tudor Williams, the founder of the Williams Bros. business, passed away at West Wales General Hospital, aged 52.

'Tudie' was laid to rest at St Michaels Churchyard, St Clears, on Saturday, 22nd December, 1973, after a service at St Martin's Church, Laugharne.

At this point in time, however, there was a steady decline in passenger loadings, so the company decided to withdraw their Sunday service between Carmarthen and Pendine. The mandatory notification of withdrawal was submitted on 7th November, 1973.

In 1973, a comparatively new operator to the area, W.J. Lewis (Lewis Coaches), Whitland, revived a former Western Welsh service from Whitland to Carmarthen (Weds & Sats only), with no objections. Mindful of this he asked for a modification to the licence in July 1974, to which Tudor Williams, Geoffrey Nicholas Jones, of Bancyfelin, and The South Wales Transport Co, all objected, but the modification was granted.

Another comparatively 'new' operator to the area, G.N. Jones, mentioned above, took over operation of the Carmarthen to Llangynog service from Williams Bros. in June 1974, but Williams Bros. didn't surrender their licence for that route TGR 457/3, until March 1975.

On 28th August, 1974, the company applied for two more Workers' Express Carriage licences as follows:-

TGR 457/19   **Saundersfoot** to **Pendine (Proof & Experimental Establishment)**
via: Fountain Head, Ridgeway, Wiseman's Bridge, and Amroth.
Mondays to Fridays.
Only workers employed at the P & E E to be conveyed on this service.
The employees will contribute towards the cost of their conveyance in accordance with a Travel Assistance Scheme.

TGR 457/20   **St Clears (Railway Station)** to **Pendine (P & E E)**
via Laugharne, Broadway, Brook and Llanmilo.
Mondays to Fridays.
Only workers employed at the P & E E to be conveyed on this service.
The employees will contribute towards the cost of their conveyance in accordance with a Travel Assistance Scheme.

The following short period licences were issued to operate the above services immediately:-

TGR 457/Sp/15   **Saundersfoot** to **Pendine (P & E E)**.
Period of operation: 2/9/1974 to 27/10/1974.

TGR 457/Sp/16   **St Clears** to **Pendine (P & E E)**.
Period of operation: 2/9/1974 to 27/10/1974.

The full term licences TGR 457/19 and TGR 457/20, were granted in November 1974.

Above: This former Trent Motor Traction (820), **FCH 20**, was a 1954 Leyland 'Tiger Cub' PSUC1/1, with Weymann 'Hermes' B44F bodywork. It was purchased from Daniel Jones & Sons Ltd, Carmarthen (4) in January 1974, and only operated for 12 months, before it was laid up, and eventually sold for scrap in August 1976. *(V. Morgan collection).*

Above: LDB 712, was a Leyland 'Tiger Cub' PSUC1/2T, with Burlingham 'Seagull' C41F coachwork, purchased from Contract Bus Services Ltd, in February 1974, but it never operated with Williams Bros. It was sold for scrap by August 1976. This view of **LDB 712** was taken when it operated for Hill's, Tredegar. See photograph on page 87 also. *(V. Morgan collection).*

Above: Williams Bros. acquired this 1961 Ford 'Thames' 402E minibus, **YTH 326**, from agricultural contractor and PSV minibus operator, W.C. Edwards, of Henfwlch Road, Carmarthen, in early 1975, for a school contract. Its eleven seat Martin Walter bodywork was down seated to seven, to comply with non PSV regulations. *(V. Morgan collection).*

Above: The long awaited bus station at Blue Street, Carmarthen opened on 3rd August, 1975, eliminating traffic congestion at Lammas Street, and centralising bus services at the new interchange. Pictured at the new bus station in 1975, is Williams Bros.' newly acquired Marshall bodied AEC Reliance, **770 NJO**, fully laden, and accompanied by Jones 'Ffoshelig' Bedford YRQ, STH 800K. **770 NJO** was new to City of Oxford MS, but was acquired via Irvine, Law, South Lanarkshire, in May 1975.

Above: On 1st April, 1974, Carmarthenshire County Council amalgamated with the neighbouring counties of Pembrokeshire and Cardiganshire to form one county renamed Dyfed. One of the first assignments the newly formed Dyfed C.C. embarked upon was a much needed bus interchange, seen above, which opened on 3rd August, 1975. Redevelopment of this area, from July 1997 to March 1999, to incorporate the Greyfriars Shopping Centre, made the bus station far smaller!   *(V. Morgan).*

Above: This view of AEC Reliance, **770 NJO**, shows it receiving maintenance on the pits, alongside the former North Western Leyland Tiger Cub, **LDB 712**, which was never operated by the company. Also see page 85.   *(V. Morgan collection).*

Above: March 1976, saw the first Leyland 'Leopard' in the Williams Bros.' stable. **ACU 301C** was a PSU3/3R model, fitted with Plaxton 'Panorama I' C49F coachwork. New to Hall Bros. South Shields, in April 1965, it was acquired via Barton Transport, Chilwell, Notts (1164). This view was taken at King St, Laugharne, on 13th February, 1977. *(V. Morgan).*

On 17th August, 1976, Alderman Tudor Williams, entrepreneur and driving force behind the Williams Bros. establishment, sadly passed away at the age of 85.

The funeral was held on Saturday 21st August, 1976, firstly with a service at his home, followed by a service at St Martin's Church, Laugharne, before burial at St Mary's Church, Llanfihangel-Abercowin, St Clears. Tudor was laid to rest in a grave next-but-one to his only son Tudor 'Tudie', who had passed away in December 1973.

The family were joined by a huge number of relatives and friends, together with Williams Brothers employees, and civic dignitaries. Both churches were overflowing, with several people paying their respects outside.

An emotional tribute to Alderman Tudor Hurst Fleming Williams was published in a local newspaper immediately after his death, which read:-

Mr Tudor Williams.

The death occurred at his home last week, of Mr. Tudor Williams, The Cottage, Victoria Street, Laugharne.

Mr. Williams, aged 85, was a prominent businessman in the area, and 50 years' ago, set up the 'Pioneer' bus company in Laugharne, and during the 1930s, he was instrumental in bringing electric to the town.

Mr. Williams also devoted a lot of his time to local government, and was a member and former Portreeve of Laugharne Corporation.

In 1955, he became a member of Carmarthen County Council, and was made an Alderman in 1937. He retired from the County Council in 1970.

Mr. Williams is survived by his wife, Mrs. Patti Williams, to whom sympathy is extended.

The funeral took place last Saturday, at St. Mary's Church, Llanfihangel-Abercowin.

Following a service at the house, conducted by the vicar of Laugharne, Reverend Iorwerth Thomas, a funeral service was held at St. Martin's Church, Laugharne.

Bearers were members of the staff at the Pioneer Bus Company, of which the late Mr. Williams was principle – Messrs. Bryn Woodworth, Ian Woodworth, Frank Thomas, David Thomas, Trevor John, and James John.

After the funeral service at St. Martin's Church, the coffin, preceded by the Portreeve, Alderman Cyril Roberts, and the chairman of the Township Community Council, Councillor Frank John, was borne to the Lych-gate by fellow Aldermen of Laugharne Corporation – David Harries, D. Clifford Roberts, Lieutenant-Colonel Ralph A. Tucker (DL), Dr J.H.T. Rees (JP), Emrys Davies, and the recorder, William Clement Thomas, (Clem Thomas).

Chief mourners were: Mrs. Patti Williams (wife), Mrs. Anita Williams (daughter-in-law), Mr & Mrs Markham Howells, Paul & Jason Rees (great grandchildren), Mrs. E. Rees (grandmother), Mr. & Mrs. R. Williams & family, Mr Colin Williams, Mr. & Mrs. Ivan Caley & family, Mrs. Dilys Williams and Mr. John Williams, Mr. & Mrs. Dennis Jump (nephews & nieces), Mr. & Mrs. Billy Lawrence, Mr. & Mrs. John Williams, Miss. M. Davies and Mr. Lewis Rees (cousins), Mervyn Howells (close friend).

The family thank relatives and friends for sympathy and kindness shown to them during the illness and death of Alderman Tudor Williams.

Dated 27th August 1976.

<u>Correction to the above account:</u> The 'Laugharne Electric Supply' was introduced by Tudor Williams and his brothers in the late 1920s.

<u>Note:</u> Tudor's cousin, Billy Lawrence, was married to one of the Ebsworth family!

Above left: Alderman Tudor Williams' grave at St Mary's churchyard, St Clears, where his wife Patti joined him in July 1992.
Above right: Tudor Williams' son, Tudor Evelyn Williams ('Tudie'), is buried in a grave next-but-one to his father, and Tudie's wife Anita, joined him there in May 2010. *(V. Morgan collection).*

Sadly, Tudor was the last partner of the Williams Brothers partnership to pass away. After his death, the business passed to his daughter-in-law Anita Williams and Anita's married daughters, Dawn Howells and Faith Rees, who were ably assisted by the garage foreman/engineer, David Thomas, and Dawn's son Max Howells.

2nd February, 1977, was another very sad day for everyone involved in the Williams Bros. business. The company's 1965 AEC Reliance, DJG 627C, suffered from brake fade as it descended Pendine Hill, carrying workmen to the Proof & Experimental Establishment, at Llanmilo. Sadly, the driver/mechanic, Bryn Woodworth, lost his life in this horrific accident, when the bus crashed through the 2ft wide sea wall, ending up on its roof on Pendine Sands. Several passengers were critically injured in the accident, and one passenger later died from his injuries. The driver was highly praised for his actions in order to save his fellow passengers, and consequently a monumental plaque was built into the repaired sea wall as a tribute to him. A picture of the plaque can be seen on page 93.

Immediately after the accident, the company hired a Bristol LS5G, XHW 404, from Silcox Motor Coach Co, to cover the vehicle shortage. In the meantime, however, another Leyland 'Leopard' with Plaxton 'Panorama II' coachwork was purchased, which came from Morris Travel of Pencoed, Mid-Glamorgan,

Four months later, the business was offered for sale as a going concern, with an asking price of £60,000 which did not include their two garages. There were three interested parties, W.J. Lewis, Whitland, who only wanted part of the business. That was rejected. Geoffrey Nicholas Jones, of Bancyfelin, who was unable to raise the capital, and Jones Motors of Login, who stated the asking price was far too high, and the sale fell through.

Above: This was the scene at Pendine Beach on 2nd February, 1977, when Williams Bros.' AEC Reliance, **DJG 627C**, smashed through the two feet wide sea wall, after suffering from brake fade descending Pendine Hill. *(V. Morgan collection).*
Below: A picture of the same bus, taken after recovery and inspection at Silcox Motor Coach Co, garage, Pembroke Dock.

Above: This memorial stone, 'In memory of a gallant bus driver, Bryn Woodworth' was incorporated into the rebuild of Pendine sea wall in 1977. *(V. Morgan).*

Above: Silcox Motor Coach Co., Pembroke Dock, loaned Williams Bros. this 1956 Bristol LS5G, **XHW 404**, in February 1977, to cover a vehicle shortage after the fatal accident at Pendine. *(V. Morgan collection).*

At this particular point in time, it was rumoured that W.J. Lewis (Lewis Coaches), Whitland, were assisting the Williams family to run their business.

This issue has been thoroughly investigated and has proven to be incorrect. Elfed Lewis, a son and partner of W.J. Lewis' business, stated that they had no involvement at all with the Williams family, apart from making an unsuccessful offer to purchase *part* of the Pioneer Coaches business.

CHANGE OF OWNERSHIP

After the death of Alderman Tudor Williams, in August 1976, and his son, Tudor ('Tudie'), two years earlier in December 1973, the business passed to 'Tudie's' widow, Anita Williams and her two daughters, Dawn Howells and Faith Rees.

Anita was also the proprietor of Laugharne Pottery.

In June 1977, another 'new' licence was asked for, but the business at this point was still operating under the old title: Tudor Williams, Brother, & Son (by then all deceased):-

TGR 457/21   **Meidrim** to **Pendine (P & E E)** via St Clears, Laugharne, and Llanmilo.
Workers stage carriage service.   *Granted 24/8/1977.*

The new management had not informed the Traffic Commissioners of the change of ownership and title. That took place in December 1977, and curiously, the Traffic Commissioners did not issue a new operator identification number, which was normal practice after a change of entity. The original identification number TGR 457, continued with the new title: **Pioneer Coaches (A.M. Williams, D.T. Howells & F. Rees, t/a).**

However, there was no outwardly difference to the business or vehicles, with the exception of a change of fleet-name to **Pioneer of Laugharne**, as seen in the photograph below.

Above: This elderly 1958 Bedford SB1, **UAX 639**, which had been owned by Williams Bros. since 1961, transferred to the new partnership of 'Pioneer Coaches' in December 1977, and was withdrawn a year later.   *(V. Morgan).*

Above: This Bedford SB5, **110 ACA**, with Duple 'Midland' B40F bodywork, also passed to the new owners of the business in December 1977. It was withdrawn from service in October 1980, and passed with the business to Jones of Login, for spares. *(Eric Wain)*.

Above:, Another vehicle transferred from Williams Bros. to Pioneer Coaches in December 1977, was former City of Oxford Motor Services, AEC Reliance, **770 NJO**. It was part exchanged in October 1978, for two Plaxton 'Derwent' bodied Ford R192s at Paul Sykes (dealer), Carlton, but soon afterwards passed to A. Barraclough (breaker), Carlton, and scrapped. *(D.S. Giles)*.

<u>Above:</u> Plaxton 'Panorama' bodied Leyland 'Leopard' PSU3/3R, **ACU 301C**, was another coach transferred from the Williams Brothers fleet in December 1977. This one also passed to Jones of Login, but was used as a source of spare parts. *(V. Morgan).*

<u>Above:</u> **ULK 204F** was another Plaxton 'Panorama' bodied Leyland 'Leopard' PSU3A/4R, transferred from Williams Bros.

Above: Last but not least, this Bedford SB5, **475 JHO**, was also transferred from Williams Bros. in December 1977, but was withdrawn from service three months later. *(V. Morgan collection).*

Above: This Plaxton 'Panorama' bodied Leyland 'Leopard' PSU3/3R, **MGA 748E**, was purchased by the new management in December 1977, from J.D. Cleverly (Capital Coaches), Pontypool. It is seen here at Sophia Gardens, Cardiff, operating a private charter, on a very snowy day, 18th February, 1978. *(V. Morgan).*

Above: GDE 375L was a grant specification Bristol LH6L, with Plaxton 'Panorama Elite III' Express body, acquired from Silcox Coaches, Pembroke Dock, in March 1978. Five months later, it was part exchanged for a Ford R1114, at Arlington's, Bristol.

Above: Captured here at Carmarthen on 12th August, 1978, is **FNN 279D**, a Bedford VAM14 with Duple 'Bella Venture' C43F coachwork, purchased by the new management from R.T. Jones, Cwmann, Lampeter, in April 1978. *(V. Morgan).*

However, one source of historical information stated that the business was incorporated in March 1978, but extensive searches by 'Companies House' staff could not find any record of a business named Pioneer Coaches Ltd., which suggests that it was not incorporated.

Additionally, the Traffic Commissioners referred to the business continuously as 'Pioneer Coaches', beginning in December 1977, when the company asked for a fare increase.

The reformed business, 'Pioneer Coaches' applied for their first road service licence in February 1978, a workmen's short period licence:-

TGR 457/Sp/17   **Meidrim** to **Pendine (P & EE)**, for period 24/2/1978 to 20/4/1978.

However, it came as a huge surprise in June 1978, when the partnership asked for a 'new' Excursions & Tours licence, the first one since the outbreak of WW2 in 1939. Nevertheless, private hire *had* been operated by the company on a very unique basis, as mentioned earlier. Tudor Williams would make his buses available to private groups with no charge whatsoever, but stipulated that the organiser must give the driver a tip, sufficient to cover his wages. This licence application read:-

TGR 457/22   **Excursions & Tours** starting from **Laugharne (Pioneer Garage)**, with pick-ups at Pendine (PO), Llanmilo (PO), St Clears (Car Park), and Meidrim (New Inn). *Max number of vehicles to be operated on a proposed group of excursions in one day to be 8. Max number of vehicles to operate on one Excursion or Tour, on any one day to be 3.   Granted 18/10/1978.*

A short period licence was issued immediately to operate the said Excursions & Tours:-

TGR 457/Sp/18   **Excursions & Tours** starting from **Laugharne (Pioneer Garage)**. Period of operation: 19/6/1978 to 13/8/78.

A month later, 26th July, 1978, the following stage carriage service licence was applied for:-

TGR 457/23   **Laugharne (The Grist)** to **Tenby (Upper Park Road)**.
via: A4066 to Pendine, B4314 and unclassified road to Marros, Amroth, Wiseman's Bridge, and Woodside, B4316 to Saundersfoot, and A478 to Tenby, via Greenhill Road, South Parade and Upper Park Road.
The service is to run in summertime only, on Mon, Tue, Thu and Fri.

The following short period licence was issued for the above Laugharne to Tenby service:-

TGR 457/Sp/19   **Laugharne (The Grist)** to **Tenby (Upper Park Road)**.
Period of operation: 27/7/1978 to 24/9/1978.

TGR 457/23 was granted on 21st March, 1979, with a condition that no passengers be picked up or set down within the Saundersfoot and Tenby section. Passengers to be picked up and set down without restriction between Marros Church and Saundersfoot only.

<u>Above:</u> This ECW bodied Bristol LS5G, **RWW 985**, was pictured at Carmarthen bus station, working the Carmarthen-Pendine service in May 1978. It was on hire from Silcox, Pembroke Dock, and was still displaying a Silcox destination blind.

<u>Above:</u> Bristol LS5G, **OTT 50**, was another vehicle hired from Silcox Motor Coach Co. Ltd., in July 1978. *(Authors collection).*

Above: Another Silcox vehicle hired by Pioneer Coaches was this Bristol MW5G, **520 JHU**, from July to August 1978.

Above: HNM 926N was a Ford R1114 with Duple 'Dominant I' Express coachwork, purchased in August 1978. It was new to R.I. Davies, Tredegar, in March 1975, passing to Stonnis, Tredegar, in February 1977 and Llynfi, Maesteg in June 1977.

Above: In October 1978, two former Midland Red (6301/2) Ford R192, with Plaxton 'Derwent' B45F bodies were purchased. Numerically the first, **YHA 301J,** is seen at Duncan Street, Laugharne, across the road from Market Lane garage. *(V. Morgan).*

Above: Numerically the second former Midland Red, Plaxton 'Derwent' bodied Ford R192 acquired by Pioneer Coaches, was **YHA 302J,** which is pictured here laid up and undergoing accident repairs in June 1979. It is parked in St Martins Church car park, Laugharne, a regular parking area used by the company for vehicles out of service. *(V. Morgan collection).*

Above: This Bedford YMT, with Plaxton 'Supreme Express' C53F coachwork, **UDE 351T**, was quite a breakthrough for the new owners of the business. Delivered in November 1978, it was the first and only 'Grant Aided' vehicle acquired by Pioneer Coaches, or their predecessors. The original proprietor, Tudor Williams, must have been 'unique' as he never took up the governments 'New Bus Grant' offer introduced in 1968, and had not bought a 'new' vehicle since January 1949. *(V. Morgan).*

Left: This Ford R192, **MHR 382F**, with Duple 'Viceroy' C45F coachwork was acquired from Tedd, (Kingston Coaches), Winterslow, near Salisbury, Wiltshire, in December 1978, but was not operated. It was passed off to Moseley (dealer) at Kilkenny, in the Republic of Ireland by July 1979, and sold to Campbell (Fingal Coaches), Dublin, in July 1979.

(V. Morgan collection).

On 2nd May, 1979, the company applied for another new stage carriage licence, which was basically a modification of an existing licence:-

TGR 457/24 **Laugharne (The Grist) to Carmarthen (Bus Station).**
via: St Clears, and Meidrim. *Wednesday and Saturday only.*
Should this licence be granted, TGR 457/11 will be surrendered.

TGR 457/24 was granted on 14th November, 1979, and TGR 457/11 was surrendered as stated, immediately afterwards.

An interesting development came about in November 1979, when the Transport Minister, Mr Norman Fowler announced details of the Road Traffic Act 1980. This Act, which came into effect on 1st October, 1980, was basically the beginning of deregulation, allowing Express Carriage services over 30 miles in distance to be freed from licensing regulations, with Excursions and Tours not requiring licensing at all.

It also abolished the licensing of bus conductors from 19th May, 1980, and reduced the minimum age for PSV (later PCV) drivers from 21 to 18, with a restriction that under 21s may only drive a PSV within a 30 mile radius of their base.

The Act also brought about the new 'coloured' operator licence discs, indicating National (Blue), International (Green), and Restricted/Special restricted (Orange). At the same time, operator identification numbers were changed from TGR xxxx to PG xxxx prefix (in the SWTA), with other traffic areas following suit with their appropriate traffic area letters.

As time progressed, the business was beginning to get too much for the new owners, Anita Williams and her daughter Dawn Howells, especially after introduction of the Road Traffic Act 1980, so they reluctantly decided it was time to sell the business.

There was an asking price of £60,000 for the eight vehicles, together with their seven stage carriage licences, workers contracts, and school contracts. The two garage premises were not included in the sale.

Arwel Jones of Jones Motors (Login) Ltd, Login, near Whitland, made an offer of £40,000. He was taking into consideration the age and condition of the vehicles, but his offer was rejected.

Haggling then commenced between the two parties, and eventually an agreement was accomplished in December 1980, when Arwel Jones offered £50,000 for the business.

The business passed to Jones Motors (Login) Ltd, on 1st January, 1981.

The following week, a local newspaper published an anthology of the Pioneer business, which is reproduced *with corrections,* on the next page:-

'BUS PIONEERS AT THE END OF THE ROAD'

'After being in operation for 72 years, one of the true 'pioneers' of public transport in West Wales has finally come to the end of the road.

For the Pioneer Bus Company, one of the oldest, best known and best-loved of Welsh bus companies has been taken over by Jones Motors of Login, Whitland.

Founded in 1908, by the late Tudor Williams, the Laugharne based firm remained a family firm throughout its long history, and up until the last few days was run by Mr Williams' daughter-in-law, Mrs Anita Williams, and grand-daughter, Mrs Dawn Howells.

However, Mrs Williams and her daughter, Dawn, found that the work involved in running the company was getting too much for them, and it was with sad hearts that they agreed to call 'Fares Please' for the last time, and handed over to the new company on New Year's Day, 1981.

Passengers on Pioneer's buses will be glad to know that the new company will continue to operate the same tri-angle of services formed between Carmarthen, Meidrim, St Clears, Laugharne and Pendine.

The drivers and eight buses will be kept on by Jones Motors, but will operate from their Login depot.

The passing of Pioneer Buses has obviously brought back a flood of fond memories to Mrs Anita Williams, whose husband, 'Tudie' (Tudor Williams junior), also worked in the firm, and died shortly before his father, in December 1973.

At her home, Lahore Cottage, Laugharne, Mrs Williams recounted the history of Pioneer Buses, and spoke of how Tudor Williams started his first scheduled run on 5th June, 1908.

Tudor Williams senior, who later became Portreeve of Laugharne, and an Alderman, was regarded as one of the 'characters' of the town, and must have cut an imposing figure on those early journeys in his favourite attire of breeches and boots.

In those early days, Tudor Williams could not be described as a bus driver, in the true sense of the word because his only transport was a six seat horse drawn wagonette or 'brake'.

Competition between the transport firms at this particular time was very keen, but Tudor managed to firmly establish himself on the route between Laugharne and the busy St Clears Station, five miles away.

He was lucky enough in 1913 to be given the contract to carry the Royal Mail, and by 1916, the business was becoming so successful, that he was also operating a coach and four horses.

Things looked very bleak for Tudor when WW1 broke out, as the Army commandeered his horses for use by the country's troops, but he bought two model TT Fords, and by using his own petrol ration, and borrowing petrol from the family doctor he survived.

For the next two years he continued to use his Ford TT's and at the end of the war he bought a Napier chassis, upon which he built his own body, and started to build up the business again.

He later bought a former troop carrier of Thornycroft manufacture, and a Ford TT bus to develop 'Laugharne Motor Services', as the business was known then.

Shortly afterwards, the company name was changed to 'Pioneer', and by the end of the 1920s, the firm was well established, operating services to Pendine, St Clears, Carmarthen and Tenby.

Tudor's wife who is now nearly 89, stated that he was greatly helped during this period, by his brothers, Ebie and Billie, when they joined the business, and of course in later years his son 'Tudie' also helped him at the wheel.

Amazingly, Tudor still took an active part in the business at the age of 80 in 1971, and twice weekly got behind the wheel of a 29 seat bus, and drove between Laugharne and Meidrim to pick up people that wanted to go into Carmarthen on market days.

By this time, Tudor carried the title of the oldest bus driver in Britain, and his daughter-in-law recalls that the Meidrim run was his favourite route. "The old man used to call it the Wells Fargo run because it went out into the wilds, and it was such a lot of fun."

The passing of Pioneer Buses has also stirred up affection among the people of Laugharne. Laugharne's Portreeve, Alderman W.S. Lewis commented that it was a sad event, and that the company had provided an excellent service to the people of the area'.

He said, "no-one knows better than the people of Laugharne what this means. Whenever anyone wanted a favour, who better to ask than Alderman Tudor Williams".

"His buses were available anytime to go anywhere, and very often for no charge whatsoever. The only stipulation was that you gave the driver a tip". He added: "I feel that Laugharne and the surrounding area owe a great debt to the bus company which now ceases to exist. As the saying goes, you never miss these things until they are gone."

THE SAD DEMISE OF PIONEER

On Thursday 1ˢᵗ January, 1981, Jones Motors (Login) Ltd., officially took control of the old established family business, 'Pioneer Coaches', Laugharne. All members of staff, excluding management, transferred to Jones Motors under the Transfer of Undertakings (Protection of Employment) regulations.

Eight vehicles transferred to Jones Motors with the Pioneer business, together with all stage carriage services, works contracts and school contracts. Two of the eight vehicles transferred to Jones Motors', Bedford - 110 ACA, and AEC Reliance - ACU301C, were not serviceable, and not operated by Jones. They were used for spare parts.

Control of the former Pioneer services, and maintenance of all vehicles was centralised at Jones' headquarters in Login.

The fleet-name 'Pioneer Coaches' was abandoned, and Pioneer's garages at Market Lane and King Street, Laugharne, were retained by the Williams family.

Market Lane garage was converted into a shop in 1981, by Anita Williams (former proprietor of Pioneer Coaches), for her Pottery business. The Pottery shop later closed down, and was converted into a restaurant known as 'The Portreeve', still owned by a descendant of the Williams family – Max Howells, a great-grandson of Alderman Tudor Williams.

The stage carriage services, workers services, and school contracts transferred to Jones Motors were:-

PG 457/2	Carmarthen to Pendine via Laugharne.	which became	PG 5052/13
PG 457/23	Laugharne to Tenby via Pendine and Amroth.	" "	PG 5052/18
PG 457/24	Laugharne to Carmarthen via Meidrim.	" "	PG 5052/19
PG 457/19	Saundersfoot to Pendine (P & EE) workers	" "	PG 5052/16
PG 457/16	Tenby to Pendine (P & EE) workers.	" "	PG 5052/15
PG 457/14	Whitland to Pendine (P & EE) workers.	" "	PG 5052/14
PG 457/21	Meidrim to Pendine (P & EE) workers.	" "	PG 5052/17
Schools	Pendine to Whitland Grammar School.		
Schools	Laugharne to Whitland Grammar School.		
Schools	Laugharne to 3 x Carmarthen Schools.		

Jones Motors applied in advance for Pioneer Coaches' licences, and were issued with the temporary short term licences listed below, for the period 17th December 1980, to 16th June 1981, in order to continue operating the services:-

PG 5052/Sp/9   **Saundersfoot** to **Pendine (P & EE)**. Workmen's stage carriage.

PG 5052/Sp/10   **Tenby** to **Pendine (P & EE)**. Workmen's stage carriage.

PG 5052/Sp/11   **Laugharne** to **Tenby**, via Pendine & Amroth. Stage carriage.

PG 5052/Sp/12   **Carmarthen** to **Pendine**. Stage carriage.

PG 5052/Sp/13   **Whitland** to **Pendine (P & EE)**. Workmen's stage carriage.

PG 5052/Sp/14   **Meidrim** to **Pendine (P & EE)**. Workmen's stage carriage.

PG 5052/Sp/15   **Laugharne** to **Carmarthen** via Meidrim. Stage carriage.

The full term licences, PG 5052/13 to 19, listed on page 109, were issued in June 1981.

Arwel Jones, the company's MD, quickly set about replacing most of the Pioneer stock, and repainted only two into fleet livery. As stated earlier, 110 ACA and ACU 301C were not used, FNN 279D was withdrawn within 3 months, Fords YHA 301/2J were gone within 6 months, HNM 926N was withdrawn within 14 months, and Leyland MGA 748E pictured below, had gone within 2 years. Bedford UDE 351T, actually saw 16 years' service.

Above: Former Pioneer Coaches, Leyland 'Leopard' PSU3/3R, **MGA 748E**, with Plaxton 'Panorama' C47F coachwork, seen here between school duties, actually received Jones Motors' livery, but left the fleet in 1983.   *(V. Morgan collection).*

Above: The newest vehicle Jones Motors acquired with the Pioneer Coaches business, was **UDE 351T**, a 'grant aided' Bedford YMT, with Plaxton 'Supreme Express' coachwork. It received this new Plaxton 'Supreme IV' front end, and was fully refurbished under a special offer introduced by Plaxton in 1982, and is seen here in Carmarthen, on 2nd April, 1983. An original view of this coach can be found on page 104. *(V. Morgan).*

Above: UDE 351T is seen here at Login, still operational on 7th April, 1996, repainted into their later style of livery. *(V. Morgan).*

Above: Manned by a former Pioneer driver, this 'grant aided' Bedford YMT, **HBX 972X**, with Duple 'Dominant II' bus bodywork, was bought by Jones, Login in August 1981, to replace former Pioneer stock. It is seen here at Carmarthen bus station in August 1981, when it was brand new, working the Carmarthen - Pendine service, newly route numbered 222. *(V. Morgan).*

Above: A later purchase by Jones, for the Carmarthen - Pendine service was **D727 GDE**, a Scania K92, with East Lancs B59F bodywork, pictured at Carmarthen when new in March 1987, before receiving its destination blind. *(V. Morgan).*

Finale

Throughout the generations, Laugharne and Pendine residents have been faithfully served with several modes of public transport.

The earliest record of passenger carriers in those communities is 1895, which stated that Henry Hitchings, Richard Pearce, and Evan David were running an infrequent 'pony and trap service' to and from St Clears Railway Station, until Tudor Williams came along in June 1908, with a regular horse-drawn service.

Tudor made history. The Williams family served the communities with a regular passenger service for no less than 72 years, which is a record.

They were challenged by Ebsworth Bros. for 35 years, and ran jointly with Western Welsh for 17 years, finally taking over Western Welsh's share of the service in 1971.

Jones Motors of Login, took the 'reigns' in January 1981, and ran the 222 Carmarthen - Pendine service faithfully for almost ten years, until August 1990, when the 'Badgerline' subsidiary, South Wales Transport, literally 'stole' the service from them, under the new deregulation laws, tendering a ridiculously low price to the local authority.

Badgerline Holdings PLC, merged with Grampian Regional Transport in April 1995, creating a brand new group called First Bus PLC.

First Bus PLC, initially retained the South Wales Transport title for their South Wales area operations, but in 1998, the South Wales Transport (SWT) title was discontinued in favour of First Cymru Buses Ltd.

From April 1998, the 222 Carmarthen - Pendine service was operated by First Cymru Buses Ltd.

In November 2009, however, Rhodri Evans, of Ffoshelig Coaches, Carmarthen, decided to register the service and compete against First Cymru Buses. First Cymru Buses were not prepared to accept a challenge on the route and immediately stood down, handing the service to Ffoshelig Coaches, who then claimed the financial support available to run it.

Thirteen months later, Ffoshelig Coaches gave the obligatory notice to terminate the 222, Carmarthen-Pendine service, due to a huge reduction in concessionary fare reimbursement from the Welsh Assembly, and a reduction in subsidies from the local authority.

Alternatively, Taf Valley Coaches (Bysiau Cwm Tâf), Whitland, took over the service on 21st February, 2011, and are currently still working the service in September 2022.

This publication is a tribute to everyone involved in the making of Laugharne's public transport history, especially Alderman Tudor Williams, who was a man of acumen in his business affairs.

Above: The Portreeve Restaurant and Tafarn at Market Lane, Laugharne, still has the character and appearance of its origins back in 1908. The building was originally Tudor Williams' stables, housing his horses and wagonette, but was converted into a garage when he turned to the modern 'mechanical mode' of transport in 1916, becoming the original Pioneer bus garage. It remained in use as such until 1980, when it was converted into a Pottery shop by Tudor Williams' daughter-in-law, Mrs Anita Williams. After closure of the shop, the premises passed to Alderman Tudor Williams' great grandson, Max Howells, who converted it into this charming, colourful restaurant, which has bags of character and excellent food. *(V. Morgan collection).*

Above: This was Williams Brothers' second garage, located at King St, Laugharne, rebuilt from Brown's Hotel Garage 1945/6. It housed 6 buses until 1980, and then became derelict, before demolishion to make way for a new house. See opposite.

Above & below: This stunning Georgian style, 6 bedroom, 6 bathroom house, with all the benefits of modern construction and parking for 6 cars, has recently been built on the site of Pioneer Garage, and is appropriately named 'Pioneer House'.

Recollections of the 'Pioneer' business - from the general public:

Dylan Thomas, the renowned poet, was a regular passenger on Pioneer's Buses, when he travelled between Swansea and his adopted Laugharne. He always sat on the downstairs back seat for the duration of his journey, and was usually inebriated.

Tudor's son, Tudor junior ('Tudie'), also worked in the business, and regularly drove the buses between Pendine and Carmarthen. On a hot day, 'Tudie' would leave the sweltering cab of his bus upon arrival at Lammas Street, Carmarthen, and pop-in to the Drovers Arms (adjacent to the bus stop), for a liquid refreshment.

One of the company's drivers, Trevor John, known affectionately as 'Benghazi' because of his soldiering service in North Africa, proudly boasted "I'll always get thee home". At one Cardiff Rugby International, when other coaches were forced off the road in a snowstorm, Trevor lived up to his boast. His coach was the only one to make it home that night. However, in mysterious circumstances, it is alleged that he once lost a double decker briefly, to a pond somewhere in Pembrokeshire.

In a very embarrassing situation, the company's hearse broke down en-route to a funeral, and was towed to the church by a tractor.

On another occasion, a driver failed to turn up for his shift. Tudor then ordered the garage 'handyman/labourer' to take the bus out on service. The labourer replied, "But I haven't got a licence to drive a bus Tudor!" To which Tudor answered, "Never mind, you'll be all right.", so off goes the handyman with the bus. Down the road, a local policeman saw him, recognised him, stopped him, and 'nicked' him for not having a PSV driving licence. A short while later, the labourer was summoned to appear in court in Laugharne. The Magistrate was Alderman Tudor Williams, who fined him £1.

One particular day, the company hired a coach from Silcox Motor Coach Company which developed a fault before leaving. A fitter from Silcox was called upon to rectify the fault, and afterwards, Tudor invited him into his office, which was amazingly across the road from the garage, in the bar of Brown's Hotel, owned by Tudor's brother Ebie, a partner in the business. Tudor's 'office' was a table, chair, and filing cabinet in the corner of the bar.

Finally, my sister-in-law, Ann, who is a 'Laugharnee', recalls the day when she fell out through an open doorway of a 'Pioneer' school bus, as it turned the corner from Gosport Street, Laugharne, into Stoneway Road (Orchard Park).

Fond memories. Happy days!

VEHICLE DETAILS - WILLIAMS BROS. (PIONEER BUSES)

Reg No	Chassis make & type	Chassis number	Body make & type	Seating	Date new	Remarks / Additional Information Previous Owner	Date acquired	Date withdrawn
BX 448	Humber 10/12hp		Motor car	?	6/1914	New. Licensed for Public Conveyance. (Livery: Green/Yellow).	6/1914	10/3/1917
DE 899	Ford 'T' 20hp		Motor car	5	4/1915	New. Licensed for Public Conveyance. (Livery: Black, to Grey).	4/1915	?
BX 672	Ford 'T' 20hp		Motor car	4	2/1916	New. Licensed for Public Conveyance. (Livery: Dark Blue).	2/1916	?
DE 897	Enfield				6/1915	Ex S+F Green. H'West. via C. David, Laugharne. Licensed for Public Conveyance.	7/1920	?
BX 937	Ford 'TT' 20hp u/w 15cwt		Van/Brake	10	5/1919	New.	5/1919	6/1919
BX 958	Napier 20/25hp u/w 2ton 10cwt		Charabanc		6/1919	New.	6/1919	7/1919
BX 968	Ford 'TT' 20hp		Lorry / charabanc. To charabanc only 11/1920		7/1919	New. Body built by Tudor Williams. Converted to charabanc only, 11/1920.	7/1919	?
BX 1005	Ford 'T' 20hp u/w 15cwt		Laundaulette		9/1919	New. Licensed for Public Conveyance.	9/1919	?
BX 1078	Ford 'TT' 20hp		Bus	B - -	12/1919	New.	12/1919	?
BX - - - -	Dennis		Body built by Ben Tucker & Tudor Williams.	B32 or B30	?	Ex War Department. Bought from WD compound Greenford, Middx.	1919	?
	Talbot		Conv. from ambulance by Tudor Williams	B10	1920?	Ex War Department Ambulance. Note: Talbot's were built from 1920 onwards.	?	?
BX 1224	Ford 'TT' 20hp u/w 15cwt		Passenger & Goods. Convertible body.		4/1920	New. Registered as charabanc to 11/1920. To lorry only, 11/1920.	4/1920	?
BX - - - -	Dodge (LHD)			B20F	1920	New. Purchased at Bath & West Show 1920.	1920	?
BX 1953	Thornycroft 'J' 30hp				?	Ex War Department Purchased from WD dump in Slough, 1921.	c6/1921	?
BX 3128?	Fiat 18BL		Built by Tudor Williams	B - -	?	New. Unconfirmed registration number. (see photo page 12).	c1/1923	?

Reg	Model	Chassis No	Body builder	Body type	Date	Notes	Date	Date
BX 6301	Chevrolet 23hp u/w 30cwt			B - -	10/1925	New. Licensed as a coach.	10/1925	?
BX 6626		RT2100162	Nelson Garages, Carmarthen	B14	3/1926	New. Supplied by Trevor Hopkins & Co, Nelson Garages, Carmarthen. (Livery: Red & White).	3/1926	?
BX 6751	W & G (possibly)				4/1926	New. Licensed Hackney.	4/1926	?
BX 7546	W & G 'L'	3236	Strachan & Brown	26	3/1927	New	3/1927	?
BX 8740	GMC 'T20' 23hp u/w 1ton 16cwt	203870		B14	5/1928	New. Supplied by Trevor Hopkins & Co, Nelson Garages, Carmarthen. (Livery: Purple & Grey).	5/1928	?
RP 9322	W & G 'LF'	2656	Strachan & Brown (believed to be)	B26	1926	Ex J. Meadows & Son, Barton Seagrave, Kettering, Northants.	1928	12/1935
TH 1701	Bedford WHG			14	5/1931	New	5/1931	?
CG 605	Thornycroft 'Cygnet' CDF/RC6	22253	Strachan	DP35F	10/1931	Ex Thornycroft demonstrator. Exhibited at 1931 motor show. Later retrofitted with diesel engine.	4/1932	12/1948
BX 7236	W & G 'L' u/w 3ton 16cwt	2559	Strachan & Brown	B26	9/1926	Ex Llanelly Express, 'Brynteg', Upper Tumble, Llanelly. (Livery: Blue & Cream).	1/1934	7/1936
TH 4284	Bedford WLB	109458	Duple	B20F	5/1934	New	5/1934	7/1944
TH 6817	Thornycroft 'Dainty' DF/FB4/1 u/w 3t 7cwt	25725	R.E.A.L. Carriage Works	C26F	3/1936	New	3/1936	1949
EPK 134	Dennis 'Lancet II' (oil engine)	175184	Dennis	C32F to C33F	1/1937	Ex Dennis Bros Ltd, demonstrator, Guildford. Believed to be a show model.	6/1937	10/1956
TF 7310	Leyland 'Titan' TD2 (oil engine)	130	Leyland	L24/24R	12/1931	Ex Leyland Motors demonstrator, acquired via James, Ammanford (145) as scrap, but used.	11/1944 lic-1945	12/1948
JY 5026	Leyland 'Titan' TD4c	5675	Weymann (completed by Mumford)	L24/24R	4/1935	Ex Plymouth C.T. (108) via: Green Luxury Cs, Walton-on-Thames, Surrey.	10/1946	12/1948
EWO 583	Bedford OWB	12852	Duple (utility) rebuilt with sliding windows, reseated	B32F to B28F	3/1943	Ex Ralph's Garages, Abertillery (83)	by11/1947	10/1963
JX 2301	AEC 'Regent' 8.8 litre oil engine	06612906	Roberts	H28/26R	1/1935	Ex Halifax (16)	6/1948	by6/1955
AWB 62	AEC 'Regent' petrol, to oil engine by 6/55	06612883	Park Royal	L27/26R	1934	Ex Sheffield C.T. (262) via S.J. Davies (dealer), Penygraig, Glam.	6/1948	?
CYV 207	Ford V8		Motor car / taxi		1936	Ex Private owner. London.	?	?

Reg	Chassis	Chassis No.	Body	Seating	Date	Notes	Date in	Date out
CWA 490	AEC 'Regent' 8.8 litre petrol engine	06614029	Weymann	H30/26R	5/1936	Ex Sheffield C.T. (290), via S.J. Davies (dealer), Penygraig, Glam.	8/1948	3/1955
ETH 204	Dennis 'Lance III'	107K3	D.J. Davies	H30/26R	1/1949	New. This was the last new vehicle purchased by Williams Bros.	1/1949	2/1962
CVT 676	AEC 'Regal'	0862033	Willowbrook	DP39F to 37 seats	4/1936	Ex Stoke Motors. Stoke-on-Trent.	3/1949	4/1953
GZ 1203	Bedford OWB	14283	SMT	B28F to 30 seats	7/1943	Ex Northern Ireland Road Transport Board, (W37).	10/1949	10/1955
DKG 524	Dennis 'Lancet III'	269J3	D.J. Davies	C35F	7/1947	Ex E.R. Forse. Cardiff.	12/1949	9/1961
DFM 127	Dennis 'Lancet II'	175610	Dennis	B39F	7/1938	Ordered by J.R. Lloyd. Bwlchgwyn, Wrexham, but delivered to Crosville (f/n WA1), in 1938. Acquired via Daniel Jones & Sons, Carmarthen.	12/1949 lic-3/1950	6/1957
DWW 492	Dennis 'Lancet II'	175734	Willowbrook (1942)	DP39F	11/1939	New as a van to Ripponden & District. Re-bodied in 6/1942 for Hackett, Hazel Grove, Stockport. To Davies Bros. Pencader, (f/n 27), 8/1948, from whom it was acquired in 12/1950.	12/1950	1/1960
GJ 7537	Leyland 'Titan' TD1	71395	Burlingham (1945)	H29/26R	6/1930	Ex Ebsworth Bros. Laugharne. (For more details, see Ebsworth Bros' fleet list).	by8/1951	5/1955
RD 5361	AEC 'Regent' (fitted diesel engine 1946/7).	06612471	Park Royal.	L26/25R	9/1935	Ex Reading Corpn Transport (10). via Beech's Garage (dealer) Hanley, Stoke on Trent.	3/1954	4/1958
FT 3903	N.G.T. SE6	104	Weymann	B44F to B36F	1936	New to Tynemouth & District T90. Ex Northern General (1158)	10/1954	10/1955
CU 3944	Leyland 'Tiger' TS8	16724	Brush	C30F	5/1938	Ex Lansdowne Luxury Coaches Ltd, Leytonstone London E11.	by4/1955	3/1956
CU 3948	Leyland 'Tiger' TS8	16728	Brush	C30F	5/1938	Ex Northern General (868).	4/1955	4/1959
EWM 347	Daimler CWA6	11735	Northern Counties (utility) re-seated by 1947.	H30/26R	6/1944	Ex Southport CT (59). Fitted AEC 8.8 litre engine and radiator from Williams Bros' JX 2301 by 7/58.	4/1955	5/1962
FWL 644	AEC 'Regent'	06615393	Park Royal	H28/24R	3/1938	New to City of Oxford (K119). Acquired via Northern General (1400).	5/1955	5/1959
GAW 679	Leyland 'Tiger' PS1/1	496648	Burlingham	FC35F	4/1950	New to Whittle. Highley, Salop. Acquired via Lansdowne Cs. London E11.	9/1955	6/1959
HB 5989	Dennis 'Lancet II'	175109	D.J. Davies (1945).	C35F	1936	Ex Wheatsheaf (D.J. Davies) Merthyr Tydfil. (See **Note A** below).	11/1956	12/1958

Reg	Chassis	Chassis No.	Body	Type	Date	History	In	Out
KMG 826	Leyland 'Tiger' TS8	301139	Harrington	C35F	5/1939	Ex Blackwell. Earl's Colne, Essex. (See **Note B** below).	7/1957	6/1959
CBX 960	Albion 'Valkyrie' CX13	58026D	Duple (1951)	B35F	3/1946	Ex West Wales Motors. Tycroes, Ammanford, 30.	5/1958	1/1964
FAB 463	Bedford OB f/c	28975	Plaxton	FC30F	10/1946	Ex Ward. Sidemoor, Bromsgrove. via Everton. Droitwich.	6/1958	11/1960
MPE 410	Dennis 'Lancet III'	414J3	Reading	DP35F	7/1948	Ex Safeguard. Guildford, Surrey.	10/1958 lic-1/1959	6/1967
GHN 385	Guy 'Arab I' 5LW (See **Note C** below)	FD25925	Northern Counties	L27/28R	1943	Originally United Automobile Services (GDO4). Ex Greyhound Luxury Coaches, Sheffield (23).	4/1959 lic-6/1959	7/1963
YMF 82	AEC 'Regal IV'	9822S1379	Roe	B44F	12/1952	Originally a demonstrator for AEC Ltd, Southall. Ex McGill. Barrhead, Renfrewshire.	6/1959 lic 7/1959	11/1969
HWY 956	Dennis 'Lancet III'	649J3	Burlingham	C33F	8/1949	Ex J.J. Longstaff & Sons, Mirfield, West Riding, Yorkshire.	1/1960	1/1966
UAX 639	Bedford SB1	67369	Duple 'Midland'	B42F	11/1958	Ex C.G. & I. Peake. Pontypool, Mon. via Thomas Bros. Llangadock. Carmarthenshire.	6/1961	3/1978
KOE 794	Dennis 'Lancet III'	794J3	Santus	FC33F to FC35F	3/1950	Ex L.F. Bowen. Birmingham. via Lord. Rushden, Northants.	9/1961	10/1964
FCY 766	Albion 'Venturer' CX19	60044A	Metro-Cammell	H30/26R	12/1948	Ex United Welsh Services, Swansea (966).	1/1962 lic 5/1962	9/1968
GUT 399	AEC 'Regal IV'	9821E462	Yeates	C41C	9/1951	Ex Brown's Blue Cs. Markfield, Leicestershire. via Williams & Davies, Southsea, Wrexham.	7/1962	3/1965
EAX 645	Guy 'Arab I' 6LW	FD25456	BBW (1951) Brislington Body Works.	L27/28RD	6/1942	Ex Red & White M.S. Chepstow (L242).	6/1963	1969
UMP 532	Bedford OB	113501	Duple 'Vista'	C29F	8/1949	Ex Northern Roadways. Glasgow. via Gwynne Price. Trimsaran, Carmarthenshire.	9/1963	5/1967
DTH 15	Albion 'Valkyrie' CX13	58030H	Duple 'A' rebuilt to full front by Thurgood 6/1959	FC35F	8/1947	Ex West Wales Motors. Tycroes, Ammanford, 40.	12/1963	2/1968
YRF 734	Sentinel STC6	6/44/99	Sentinel	B44F	4/1953	Ex Whieldon. Rugeley, Staffs. (45). via Lewis. Falmouth, Cornwall.	4/1965	7/1966
UEV 829	Bristol LS5G	89.004	Eastern Coach Works	B43F	12/1952	Ex Eastern National O.C. (1200).	7/1965	6/1971
FMO 939	Bristol LL6B	81.122	Eastern Coach Works	B39R	8/1950	Ex Thames Valley Traction Co (557). via United Welsh Services, Swansea (557).	12/1965	by 9/1971

Registration	Chassis	Chassis No.	Body	Seating	Date	History	In	Out
FMO 16	Bristol L6B	79.119	Eastern Coach Works	B35R	5/1950	Ex Thames Valley Traction Co (541) via United Welsh Services. Swansea (541).	2/1966	1973
SFC 501	Guy 'Arab UF' 6LW	UF71338	Lydney - finished by BBW (built to Leyland's style)	C41C	4/1953	Ex South Midland M.S. (86). via Red & White M.S. Chepstow (DS1552).	7/1966	c5/1972
JWO 221	Leyland 'Royal Tiger' PSU1/13	511310	Lydney finished by BBW (Brislington Body Works)	B45F	12/1952	Ex Red & White M.S. Chepstow (U651).	4/1967	1971
JWO 126	Leyland 'Royal Tiger' PSU1/13	505501	Lydney	C41F	6/1951	Ex Red & White M.S. Chepstow (U3851)	6/1967	6/1973
BVV 418	Bedford OB	144891	Duple 'Vista'	C29F	10/1950	Ex Wesley. Stoke Golding, Leicestershire (32). via Owen. Berriew. Montgomeryshire.	5/1967	by 5/1975
HWO 332	Guy 'Arab III' 6LW	FD70103	Duple	L27/26RD	1/1950	Ex Red & White M.S. (L949) via West Wales Motors Tycroes, Ammanford (53)	by 9/1968 lic-10/1968	8/1972
GWO 878	Guy 'Arab III' 6LW	FD36276	Duple	L27/26RD	12/1949	Ex Red & White M.S. (L249) via West Wales Motors Tycroes, Ammanford (55)	8/1969	4/1972
YWN 481	Bedford SB8	85150	Plaxton 'Embassy I'	C41F	3/1961	Ex Bryn Demery Coaches. Morriston, Swansea. via Pursey (Caerphilly Greys), Caerphilly, Glam.	11/1969	1973
OUP 662	Leyland 'Tiger Cub' PSUC1/1	542910	Saunders Roe	B44F	8/1954	Ex Sunderland & District (265). via Thomas Bros. Llangadog, Carms.	3/1971	11/1974
MUH 157	Leyland 'Tiger Cub' PSUC1/1	566495	Weymann 'Hermes'	B44F	12/1956	Ex Western Welsh O.C. (1157).	4/1971	by 3/1978
MUH 161	Leyland 'Tiger Cub' PSUC1/1	566475	Weymann 'Hermes'	B44F	11/1956	Ex Western Welsh O.C. (1161).	4/1971	8/1976
TVO 231	Leyland 'Tiger Cub' PSUC1/2T	556470	Willowbrook	DP41F	5/1956	Ex East Midlands (C31). via Thomas Bros. Llangadog, Carms.	6/1971	10/1976
662 DAB	Ford 'Thames Trader' 570E	510E63524	Duple 'Yeoman'	C41F	4/1961	Ex Jones Bros. Gt Malvern, Worcs.	by 8/1971	6/1972
110 ACA	Bedford SB5	93674	Duple 'Midland'	B40F	2/1964	Ex Williams. Ponciau, Wrexham.	by 9/1971 lic 11/1971	3/1978
UTX 9	Leyland 'Royal Tiger' PSU1/13 (See **Note D** below)	511325 (1951)	Massey (1956)	B44F	7/1956	Ex Caerphilly UDC (9). via W. Way, scrap dealer, Cardiff.	4/1972	11/1974
KEJ 639	Bedford CALV	151145	Martin Walter	11	1/1960	Ex Woodhouse. Newtown, Montgomeryshire.	by 5/1972 non PSV	?
NHE 112	Leyland 'Tiger Cub' PSUC1/1T	577384	Park Royal	B44F	1/1958	Ex Yorkshire Traction (439).	7/1972	8/1977

Registration	Chassis	Chassis No.	Body	Seating	Date	History		
SHE 173	Leyland 'Tiger Cub' PSUC1/1	596437	Metro-Cammell	B45F	6/1961	Ex Yorkshire Traction (501).	8/1972	12/1976
475 JHO	Bedford SB5	93179	Plaxton 'Embassy III'	C41F	10/1963	New to Cook. Stoughton. Ex Howsden Caldwell Cs. Loughborough.	11/1972	by 3/1978
PMW 386	Leyland 'Tiger Cub' PSUC1/2	577035	Harrington	DP41F	1/1958	New to Silver Star. Porton Down, Wilts (32). Ex Wilts & Dorset (995), via Hants & Dorset (not operated).	3/1973	by 8/1975
FCH 20	Leyland 'Tiger Cub' PSUC1/1	534835	Weymann 'Hermes'	B44F	6/1954	Ex Trent M.T. (820). via: Dan Jones. Abergwili, Carmarthen (4).	by1/1974 lic-2/1974	2/1975
LDB 712	Leyland 'Tiger Cub' PSUC1/2	574011	Burlingham 'Seagull V'	C41F	4/1957	Ex North Western Road Car Co. (712). Ex Contract Bus Services Ltd. Caerwent, Mon.	c2/1974 not lic	Not operated
YTH 326	Ford 'Thames' 402E	400E 86090	Martin Walter	11 to 7 seat	9/1961	Ex W.C. Edwards. Henfwlch Rd, Carmarthen.	by3/1975 Non PSV	by 7/1975
770 NJO	AEC 'Reliance'	4MU3RA 4401	Marshall	B53F	12/1962	New to City of Oxford M.S. (770). Ex Irvine. Law, South Lanarkshire.	5/1975	3/1978
KDA 962D	Morris J2BM		Morris	7		Ex Private owner.	by11/1975	?
ACU 301C	Leyland 'Leopard' PSU3/3R	L23998	Plaxton 'Panorama I'	C49F	4/1965	New to Hall Bros. South Shields. Ex Barton. Chilwell, Notts. (1164).	3/1976	3/1978
DJG 627C	AEC 'Reliance' 590	2U3RA 5696	Park Royal	C49F	6/1965	Ex East Kent Road Car Co.	9/1976	2/1977
KWK 703E	Ford Transit	BCO5GM 58130	Ford	12	3/1968	Ex D.D. Jones. Pandy Mill, Mydrim, Carms.	by 2/1977	3/1978
XHW 404	Bristol LS5G	117.108	Eastern Coach Works	B45F	12/1956	Hired from Silcox. Pembroke Dock 92.	2/1977	2/1977
ULK 204F	Leyland 'Leopard' PSU3A/4R	801541	Plaxton 'Panorama II'	C51F	6/1968	New to City Coach Lines, Waltham Abbey, Essex Ex Morris Travel, Pencoed, Glam.	2/1977	3/1978
MGA 748E	Leyland 'Leopard' PSU3/3RT	700370	Plaxton 'Panorama I'	C47F	5/1967	New to Cotter. Glasgow. via Cleverly (Capitol). Pontypool. Mon.	12/1977	3/1978

Note A: The chassis of HB 5989 was new to Glenton Tours, London, SE15, in 1936, on a vehicle registered CYU 917. It was purchased by D.J. Davies, Merthyr Tydfil in 1945, re-bodied in their coachbuilding department, and re-registered in July 1945. Following its 'disguise', it entered service as HB 5989 with Wheatsheaf Motors, Merthyr, a subsidiary of D.J. Davies.

Note B: KMG 826 was new to Valliant Direct Coaches, Ealing, London W5, in 5/1939. It passed to H & S in 1944, and to W. King & Sons (Enfield Coaches), London in 3/1948. It arrived at Black & White Coaches, London E17 in 5/1949, and passed to Blackwell's, Earl's Colne, Essex in 3/1954, before arriving at Williams Bros. Laugharne, in 7/1957. I recall travelling in this coach, on a round trip between Carmarthen and Pendine in January 1959. It had a musty smell of dampness!

Note C: This vehicle was actually GHN 384 masquerading as GHN 385. All identity, including chassis plates, had been interchanged on both buses at the dealer's, before sale to Williams Bros. The original GHN 385 was broken up as GHN 384.

Note D: The chassis of UTX 9, was manufactured by Leyland Motors in May 1951, and fully reconditioned by them in 1956. It was then bodied with a *new* Massey B44F body, and delivered to Caerphilly UDC, in 7/1956.

VEHICLE DETAILS - PIONEER COACHES

Reg No	Chassis Make & Type	Chassis number	Body Make & Type	Seating	Date New	Remarks / Additional Information Previous owner	Date Acquired	Date Withdrawn
BVV 418	Bedford OB	144891	Duple 'Vista'	C29F	10/1950	Ex Williams Bros. Laugharne.	3/1978 Not licenced	Not operated
475 JHO	Bedford SB5	93179	Plaxton 'Embassy III'	C41F	10/1963	Ex Williams Bros. Laugharne.	3/1978 Not licenced	Not operated
UAX 639	Bedford SB1	67369	Duple 'Midland'	B42F	11/1958	Ex Williams Bros. Laugharne.	3/1978	by 12/1978
110 ACA	Bedford SB5	93674	Duple 'Midland'	B40F	2/1964	Ex Williams Bros. Laugharne.	3/1978	by 10/1980
YTH 326	Ford 'Thames' 402E	400E 86090	Martin Walter	7	9/1961	Ex Williams Bros. Laugharne. (Non PSV).	3/1978 Non-PSV	by12/1980
KWK 703F	Ford 'Transit'	BCO5GM 58130	Ford	12	3/1968	Ex Williams Bros. Laugharne. (Non PSV).	3/1978 Non-PSV	by12/1980
770 NJO	AEC 'Reliance'	4MU3RA 4401	Marshall	B53F	12/1962	Ex Williams Bros. Laugharne.	3/1978	10/1978
ACU 301C	Leyland 'Leopard' PSU3/3R	L23998	Plaxton 'Panorama I'	C49F	4/1965	Ex Williams Bros. Laugharne.	3/1978	12/1980

MGA 748E	Leyland 'Leopard' PSU3/3R	700370	Plaxton 'Panorama I'	C47F	5/1967	Ex Williams Bros. Laugharne.	3/1978	12/1980
ULK 204F	Leyland 'Leopard' PSU3A/4R	801541	Plaxton 'Panorama II'	C51F	6/1968	Ex Williams Bros. Laugharne.	3/1978	10/1978
GDE 375L	Bristol LH6L	LH659	Plaxton 'Panorama Elite III' Express	C45F	2/1973	Ex Silcox. Pembroke Dock (120).	3/1978	8/1978
FNN 279D	Bedford VAM14	6810124	Duple 'Bella Venture'	C43F	3/1966	Ex R.T. Jones (Rhys Coaches), 'Penpompren', Cwmann, Lampeter. Ceredigion.	4/1978	12/1980
RWW 985	Bristol LS5G	117.053	Eastern Coach Works	B45F	7/1956	Hired from Silcox. Pembroke Dock.	5/1978	5/1978
520 JHU	Bristol MW5G	164.100	Eastern Coach Works	B45F	10/1960	Hired from Silcox. Pembroke Dock.	7/1978	8/1978
OTT 50	Bristol LS5G	97.139	Eastern Coach Works	B45F	1/1954	Hired from Silcox. Pembroke Dock.	7/1978	8/1978
HNM 926N	Ford R1114	BCO4PP 66800	Duple 'Dominant I' Express	C53F	3/1975	Ex R.I. Davies. Tredegar + Stonnis, Tredegar. via Llynfi Motors (dealer loan), Maesteg, Glam.	8/1978	12/1980
YHA 301J	Ford R192	BCO4KM 49873	Plaxton 'Derwent'	B45F	11/1970	Ex Midland Red (6301).	10/1978	12/1980
YHA 302J	Ford R192	BCO4KM 49874	Plaxton 'Derwent'	B45F	11/1970	Ex Midland Red (6302).	10/1978	12/1980
UDE 351T	Bedford YMT	HW455453	Plaxton 'Supreme' Express	C53F	11/1978	New	11/1978	12/1980
MHR 382F	Ford R192	BCO4GL 19940	Duple 'Viceroy'	C45F	6/1968	Ex Tedd (Kingston Cs), Winterslow, Wiltshire.	12/1978	Not operated

VEHICLE DISPOSALS - WILLIAMS BROS/PIONEER BUSES

BX 448	Registration voided 10/3/1917. Registration number re-issued 5/1917.
DE 899	No further trace.
BX 672	No further trace.
DE 897	No further trace.
BX 937	Sold to James Hughes, Trimsaran, Carms, 6/1919. To J.C. Thomas, Narberth, Pembs, 9/1920.
BX 958	Sold to E. Philpot, Newbridge, Monmouthshire, 7/1919.
BX 968	No further trace.
BX 1005	No further trace.
BX 1078	No further trace.
BX - - - -	(Dennis) No further trace.
	(Talbot) No further trace.
BX 1224	No further trace.
BX	(Dodge) No further trace.
BX 1953	No further trace.
BX 3128?	Sold to unknown Glamorganshire owner.
BX 6301	No further trace.
BX 6626	Converted into lorry, at unknown date.
BX 6751	No further trace.
BX 7546	No further trace.
BX 8740	Last licensed 1935. No further trace.
RP 9322	Last licensed 12/1935. No further trace.
TH 1701	No further trace.
CG 605	Last licensed 12/1948. No further trace.
BX 7236	Last licensed 7/1936. No further trace.
TH 4284	Sold to T. Williams. Upper Chapple, Brecon, 7/1944. Last licensed 1949.
TH 6817	Last licensed 1949. No further trace.
EPK 134	No further trace.
TF 7310	Sold to S. Eynon & Sons, Trimsaran, Carmarthenshire, 1949.
JY 5026	Sold to S. Eynon & Sons, Trimsaran, Carmarthenshire, 7/1949.
EWO 583	Scrapped 11/1963.
JX 2301	Sold to Robert Hitchcock (scrap dealer), Sandy Rd, Llanelly, minus engine and radiator, 1956.
AWB 62	No further trace.
CYV 207	No further trace.
CWA 490	Last licensed 3/1955. Sold 6/1955.
ETH 204	De-licensed 2/1962. Sold to Greenhous (dealer) Hereford, to Hampton (scrap dealer) Hereford, 12/1962.
CVT 676	No further trace.
GZ 1203	In use as a farm shed at Cross Inn, near Laugharne by July 1958, still there 1/1959.
DKG 524	No further trace.
DFM 127	Sold to unknown showman by 1957. To W. Taylor (showman) Cardiff 3/1959 to 8/1960.
DWW 492	No further trace.
GJ 7537	Sold to Lansdowne Luxury Coaches Ltd, Leytonstone, London E11, 6/1955, licenced 7/1955.
RD 5361	Scrapped 6/1958.
FT 3903	Sold to AMCC (dealer), Stratford, London E15, by 2/1956.
CU 3944	Sold to Rhymney Transport, Rhymney, Monmouthshire.
CU 3948	Sold to L. Leonard. Liverpool (Non PSV operator), 4/1959. Last licensed 1/1961.
EWM 347	Sold to W. Way (scrap dealer) Cardiff by 6/1962. Still there 1/1977.
FWL 644	Sold to a local contractor by 6/1959.
GAW 679	Sold to Hughes (dealer) Bradford, 6/1959. To Brunskill. Accrington, Lancs. 6/1959, & withdrawn 8/1959.
HB 5989	Sold 12/1958.
KMG 826	No further trace.
CBX 960	No further trace.

FAB 463	Sold to Everall (dealer), Wolverhampton, 9/1961, awaiting scrap 6/1962.
MPE 410	Sold 7/1967. No further trace.
GHN 385	Sold to Jones (scrap dealer) Cardiff 7/1963. To W. Way (scrap dealer) Cardiff 5/1966.
YMF 82	Sold to Vivienne Jean Peters, Pembrey, Carmarthenshire, 11/1969.
HWY 956	No further trace.
UAX 639	To Pioneer Coaches, Laugharne, after the company's change of ownership in 3/1978.
KOE 794	Parked up in garage, out of use, 10/1965. No further trace.
FCY 766	Sold to Arlington Motors (dealer) Cardiff by 3/1969. To Way (breaker) Cardiff by 3/1969, still there 10/1977.
GUT 399	Sold to Kirkby (dealer), South Anston, S Yorks, by 8/1965. Body to Johnson (breaker) Worksop, Notts, 1966. Chassis exported to Australia, 9/1966.
EAX 645	Sold to W. Way (breaker), Cardiff by 8/1969.
UMP 532	Derelict at depot by 7/1968. Later scrapped.
DTH 15	Sold to Woodland (dealer), Chepstow, scrapped at Newport.
YRF 734	Sold to Woodland (dealer), Chepstow. To P.J. Dolan (Shamrock Coaches), Newport, Mon. 7/1966.
UEV 829	Sold to Gardner David (dealer), Onibury, Ludlow, Salop, 6/1971.
FMO 16	Sold to Baker. Saundersfoot, (as mobile boutique) by 1/1974. To Baxter. Exeter, preservationist, at West of England Transport Collection, Winkleigh 10/1976. To Booth, Rotherham (breaker, minus engine), 9/79.
FMO 939	Sold to Moseley (dealer), Cinderford, Gloucestershire 9/1971, in part exchange for 110 ACA.
SFC 501	Sold to Greenhous (dealer) Hereford, c5/1972, in part exchange for 662 DAB. To Smith (breaker), Sutton-St-Nicholas, Hereford, 5/1972.
JWO 126	Sold 1/1973.
JWO 221	Sold to Gardner David (dealer) Ludlow, Salop, 7/1971
BVV 418	Withdrawn in 1975, passed to Pioneer Coaches as non-runner in 3/1978. Still owned in derelict condition parked in St Martins Church car park, Laugharne, 3/1980. No further trace.
HWO 332	Sold 3/1974. No further trace.
GWO 878	Sold to W. Way (breaker), Cardiff, 6/1972.
YWN 481	Gardner Diesel Exporting Co (dealer) Ludlow, Salop, 11/1973.
OUP 662	No further trace.
MUH 157	No further trace.
MUH 161	Sold to a scrap dealer at Whitland, Carmarthenshire, 10-12/1976.
TVO 231	Sold to a scrap dealer at Whitland, Carmarthenshire, 10-12/1976.
110 ACA	To Pioneer Coaches, Laugharne, 3/1978, after the company's change of ownership.
UTX 9	Sold to John Rees (breaker), Gorslas, Carmarthenshire, 7/1976.
662 DAB	Sold to Martin (dealer) Middlewich, Cheshire, by 7/1972. To Car Transporter by 7/1973.
KEJ 639	No further trace.
NHE 112	No further trace.
SHE 173	Sold to scrap dealer at Whitland, Carmarthenshire, 3/1977.
PMW 386	Sold to John Rees (breaker) Gorslas, Carmarthenshire, 7/1976.
475 JHO	To Pioneer Coaches, Laugharne, 3/1978, after the company's change of ownership, but not used.
FCH 20	Still owned 3/1976. Sold to John Rees (breaker), Gorslas, Carmarthenshire, by 8/1976.
LDB 712	Not operated. Sold to John Rees (breaker), Gorslas, Carmarthenshire, by 8/1976.
YTH 326	Operated as non PSV. Withdrawn by 7/1975.
KDA 962D	No further trace.
770 NJO	To Pioneer Coaches, Laugharne, 3/1978, after the company's change of ownership.
ACU 301	To Pioneer Coaches, Laugharne, 3/1978, after the company's change of ownership.
DJG 627C	Written off after horrific fatal accident at Pendine, 2/2/1977 (see photo page 92). Its remains were broken up at Silcox's yard, Pembroke Dock, after 6/1977.
KWK703E	To Pioneer Coaches, Laugharne, 3/1978, after the company's change of ownership.
XHW 404	Returned to Silcox Coaches, Pembroke Dock, off hire, 2/1977.
ULK 204F	To Pioneer Coaches, Laugharne, 3/1978, after the company's change of ownership.
MGA 748E	To Pioneer Coaches, Laugharne, 3/1978, after the company's change of ownership.

VEHICLE DISPOSALS - PIONEER COACHES

BVV 418	Not operated. Stored at King Street garage until 1/1980. Dumped at St Martins Church car park by 3/1980.
475 JHO	Withdrawn by 3/1978. No further trace.
YTH 326	Disused by 1/1981. No further trace.
KWK 703F	Disused by 1/1981. No further trace.
UAX 639	Out of use by 12/1978. Gone by 2/1979.
110 ACA	Withdrawn by 10/1980. Transferred to Jones, Login, with the business 1/1/1981, and used for spares.
770 NJO	Sold to Paul Sykes (dealer), Carlton, 10/1978. To A. Barraclough (breaker), Carlton by 10/1979.
ACU 301C	Transferred to Jones, Login, with the business 1/1/1981. Not operated by Jones, used for spares.
MGA 748E	Transferred to Jones, Login, with the business 1/1/1981.
ULK 204F	Sold to PSO (dealer), Barnsley, 10/1978. To Abingdon Coaches, Oxfordshire, 2/1980.
GDE 375L	Sold to Arlington (dealer), Bristol, 8/1978. To Deeble, Upton Cross, Cornwall, 6/1980.
FNN 279D	Transferred to Jones, Login, with the business 1/1/1981.
RWW 985	Returned to Silcox Coaches, Pembroke Dock, off hire, 5/1978.
520 JHU	Returned to Silcox Coaches, Pembroke Dock, off hire, 8/1978.
OTT 50	Returned to Silcox Coaches, Pembroke Dock, off hire, 8/1978.
HNM 926N	Transferred to Jones, Login, with the business 1/1/1981.
YHA 301J	Transferred to Jones, Login, with the business 1/1/1981.
YHA 302J	Transferred to Jones, Login, with the business 1/1/1981.
UDE 351T	Transferred to Jones, Login, with the business 1/1/1981.
MHR 382F	Probably not operated. Sold to Moseley (dealer), Kilkenny, Republic of Ireland, 7/1979. To Campbell (Fingal Coaches), Dublin, 7/1979.

Above: Tudor Williams' favourite coach, **BVV 418**. It was so sad to find this Bedford OB, in such a poor condition, dumped in the car park of St Martins Church, Laugharne, on 9th March, 1980. *(Vernon Morgan)*.

TICKETS USED BY WILLIAMS BROS

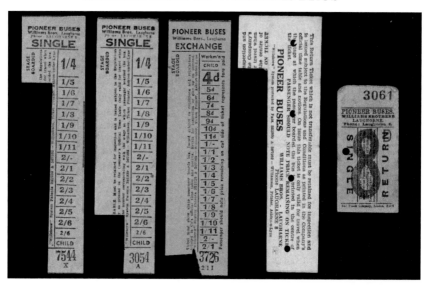

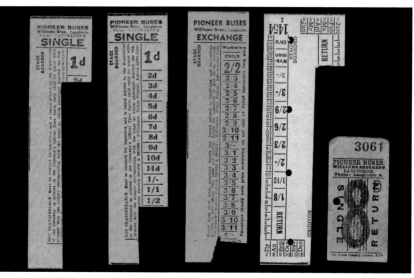

Above: A selection of Williams Bros (Pioneer Buses), Willebrew, and Bell punch bus tickets, pre-decimalisation.

EBSWORTH BROTHERS, LAUGHARNE

The Ebsworth family were well known and well respected business entrepreneurs in the village of Pendine, Carmarthenshire, during the late 19th and early 20th century.

John Stephen Ebsworth, a native of the neighbouring village, Marros, established himself in the community of Pendine as a rabbit dealer, game dealer, and animal keeper, after his marriage to Mary Elizabeth Lewis, in 1880. Mary was the daughter of David Lewis, proprietor of the famous Beach Hotel at Pendine.

In addition to managing the Beach Hotel, David Lewis also dealt in rabbits, and it's reputed that between them, they had a lucrative business. Their rabbits and game would be taken by horse and cart to St. Clears Railway Station, and loaded on to the trains for shipment to all parts of the country.

After his marriage, John Ebsworth and his wife Mary took up residence at the Beach Hotel with his in-laws, and eventually moved into what became their family home, Beach Cottage (later Seaview), situated next door to the Beach Hotel, where all their children grew up.

Above: A view of lower Pendine in 1907, with the Beach Hotel in the foreground, and Beach Cottage to its right hand side.

When their first son was born in 1880, he was given his grandfather's forename and surname, *David Lewis* Ebsworth, and when he became of age, followed in his father's footsteps with his own business – a game dealer and butcher.

A notable feature of the Ebsworth family was that the first three sons received the middle name of 'Lewis', their mother's maiden name: *David Lewis*, *Thomas Lewis* and *John Lewis*.

The first motor vehicle owned by the Ebsworth family was a second-hand Beaufort 24hp, which was registered BX 164, to John Stephen Ebsworth, the game dealer, on 7th November, 1910. By this point in time, John had become landlord of the family owned Beach Hotel.

The Beaufort was purchased to replace the horse and cart which regularly carried his goods on the 10 mile trek to St. Clears Railway Station. It was also used to convey guests to the Beach Hotel, as it had detachable bodies, changing from a wagon to a car.

Beaufort motor cars were built by the Beaufort Motor Co. Ltd., of Baker Street, London, for a short period between 1902 and 1906.

Sadly, John Stephen Ebsworth passed away in June 1911, aged 51, and was succeeded at the Beach Hotel and Beach Hotel Garage, by his eldest son David Lewis Ebsworth (Davie), the butcher and game dealer mentioned earlier.

By July 1914, John Lewis Ebsworth (Jack), was recorded as a motor dealer at the Beach Hotel, and a short while later, in February 1916, David Ebsworth purchased his first motor car. This was a 20hp Ford 'Model T' registered BX 737, which was licenced for 'public conveyance', in order to provide a taxi service for guests of the Beach Hotel.

However, shortly after the cessation of World War 1 hostilities, and peace signed with Germany, the Ebsworth brothers saw how well Tudor Williams was doing with his motor bus service to St. Clears Railway Station, which prompted them to form a partnership and challenge him on the route. The partnership was formed in early 1919, running an Austin bus named 'The Pearl', and initially consisted of all four brothers, David (Davie), Thomas (Tom), John (Jack), and Harold. Tom had returned home from the 8th Battalion Grenadier Guards, where he held the position of Lieutenant, having enlisted in the Army in 1911.

By this time, John and Tom were living at 'Fullerton House', next door to the famous Brown's Hotel, in King Street, Laugharne, which became their business' address. Tom became manager of the business, and the vehicles were garaged opposite, at Brown's Hotel Garage, which was rented from the hotel owner, Mrs Griffiths, and renamed Central Garage. In 1937, however, Tudor Williams' brother and business partner, Ebie, bought the Brown's Hotel together with its garage, resulting in the Ebsworth brothers swiftly vacating it. The Ebsworth brothers alternatively purchased an old timber yard and a garden in Clifton Street, from the Broadway Estate, where they built their new operating centre, Clifton Garage.

The vehicles acquired in 1919 to inaugurate their first service, ranged from an Austin 'twin shaft' bus to an American built 'Puritan Lyon' 20/30hp Laundaulette, registered, BX 897, acquired from D. Williams, Llanelly, which was rebuilt into a bus by the brothers, and in October 1919, a new Ford 'Model T' registered BX 1021, arrived.

In February 1920, David Ebsworth bought a new Traffic 20-25hp, 30 cwt lorry registered BX 1114, and started dabbling in road haulage. The Traffic was an American chassis, built in St Louis, Missouri, and a month later in March 1920, the brothers bought a second-hand Ford 'Model T', registered BX 1135, from Benjamin Davies, of the County Supply Stores, at St. Clears. Interestingly, Benjamin Davies was the first operator to run a passenger service between Carmarthen and Narberth, via St. Clears and Whitland, until W. Edwards & Son, (the Ford agent at Towy Garage, Bridge Street, Carmarthen), came along in November 1928, and started a jointly operated service between Carmarthen and Narberth.

A month later in April 1920, the Ford 'Model T', BX 1135, was followed by another Traffic 20-25hp, registered BX 1260. This had a charabanc body finished in French Grey, built on a goods vehicle chassis by coachbuilders, S. Jackett & Sons of Zion Row, Llanelly.

Jackett's were an established firm that built horse-drawn carriages, traps, wagonetts, etc.

The last Ford 'Model T' acquired by the Ebsworth brothers was registered BX 1432, and arrived in August 1920.

In the light of all this activity at Laugharne, their interests at Pendine were not forgotten. The family owned 'Beach Hotel' on the promenade was the centre of activity in the 1920s, when motor racing events took place on the famous 7 miles long, Pendine Sands.

BEACH HOTEL, PENDINE

CARMARTHEN

D. EBSWORTH

FIRST CLASS FAMILY HOTEL

With Large dining hall

LARGE PARTIES CATERED FOR

Hot and Cold Luncheons and teas at Moderate Terms

Above: An advertisement for the Beach Hotel, Pendine, which appeared in a local newspaper dated May 1924.

Famous names from Brooklands, Captain (later Sir) Malcolm Campbell, and John Godfrey Parry Thomas could be seen there in person, and the Ebsworth family met all the famous racing drivers and record breakers at the hotel and its garage, which was located virtually alongside the slipway to Pendine Sands. J.G. Parry Thomas always booked a suite at the

Beach Hotel, but practically lived in the hotel garage. Malcolm Campbell usually stayed in Tenby, and others would stay at the Brown's Hotel in Laugharne.

Malcolm Campbell, with his V12, 350hp, aero-engine Sunbeam, set up a new world record of 146.16 mph at Pendine, in 1924, and by March 1925, raised the record to 150.87 mph, with the Sunbeam. However, on 27th April, 1926, Parry Thomas took the record at Pendine, and the following day, 28th April, 1926, he raised it to over 170 mph – a record which stood for almost a year. The car named 'Babs' was a 'Higham Special', powered by a 27 litre, Liberty V12 aero-engine.

In February 1927, Campbell set up a new record of 174.88 mph at Pendine in his Napier-Campbell Bluebird, powered by a 23.9 litre, 12 cylinder, Napier 'Lyon' engine, which developed 500 bhp. In the meantime, Parry Thomas returned to Pendine to try and regain his own world land speed record, which had been broken 2 weeks earlier by Campbell on the same beach. Parry Thomas, the Welsh engineer, was the first driver killed in pursuit of the land speed record, on 3rd March, 1927, aged 42. Thomas was the chief engineer at Leyland Motors Ltd. *(I sometimes wonder whether the connection between Parry Thomas and Ebsworth brothers' influenced them into purchasing their first Leyland? – Author)*

However, Campbell broke his own record, and achieved 179.158 mph in February 1928.

Above: Parry Thomas in the seat of his 'Higham Special' named 'Babs', outside the Beach Hotel, Pendine, in October 1925, with David Lewis Ebsworth, first from right, and John (Jack) Ebsworth, third from right. *(Peter Jenkins collection).*

Left: This view of John Ebsworth, (left), and record breaker Parry Thomas (right), was taken on the promenade at Pendine, outside the Beach Hotel on 2nd March, 1927, a day before Parry Thomas' fatal accident on Pendine Sands.
(Peter Jenkins collection).

Above: A splendid view of Pendine Sands and its tiny promenade, with the Beach Hotel visible just left of the picture's centre. This is the seven miles of golden sands, where the land speed records were achieved in the 1920s.   *(V. Morgan collection).*

The Ebsworth brothers also formed close links with Green's Motors of Haverfordwest, in 1926, when Green's operated a service from Pembroke Dock to Carmarthen, and very briefly in 1926, ran Tenby to Carmarthen via Pendine and Laugharne, garaging their buses at Ebsworth Bros.' depot. Green's Motors even supported Ebsworth Bros. by giving them the loan of a bus when they had maintenance issues in June/July 1926. Furthermore, the youngest Ebsworth brother, Harold, left the partnership and accepted the position of manager at Green's Motors' 'Stepney Garage', at Water Street, Llanelly, in 1930.

DAILY TIMETABLE

Commencing Saturday, March 7ᵗʰ 1925

Pembroke Dock – Carmarthen.

Leave	a.m	p.m	Leave	a.m	p.m
Pier Hotel, Pembroke - Dock	8.30	3.45	Guildhall Square, Carmarthen	12.15	6.15
Milton	8.50	4.05	Bankyfelin	12.40	6.40
Cross Inn	9.05	4.20	St. Clears	12.50	6.50
Kilgetty	9.15	4.30	Llanddowror	1.00	7.00
Commercial Inn	9.25	4.40	Roses	1.15	7.15
Roses	9.45	5.00	Commercial Inn	1.35	7.35
Llanddowror	10.00	5.15	Kilgetty	1.45	7.45
St. Clears	10.10	5.25	Cross Inn	1.55	7.55
Bankyfelin	10.20	5.35	Milton	2.10	8.10
Arr. Guildhall Square, Carmarthen	10.45	6.00	Arr. Pier Hotel, Pembroke Dock	2.30	8.30

Left: A Green's Motors timetable, issued for their new daily Pembroke Dock to Carmarthen service in 1925. *(V. Morgan collection).*

GREEN'S MOTORS Ltd.

Taking into account that Carmarthen was the county town, the local authority, Carmarthen Borough Council, were late implementing their Hackney licensing duties. Discussions regarding bus control in the town had been held frequently between 1924-6, but the first licences were not issued to operators until February 1926.

However, there is no evidence that Ebsworth Bros. or Williams Bros. plied unlicensed into Carmarthen town before 1926. It appears that both operators only ran between Pendine and St Clears Railway Station, where their clientele caught trains to and from other destinations.

Tudor Williams & Brothers received their first licence to operate into Carmarthen on 24ᵗʰ February, 1926, and Ebsworth Bros. followed fourteen months later, on 19ᵗʰ April, 1927. However, knowing the background of these two operators, Carmarthen licensing committee specified that in order to prevent racing between them, the service timings of 9.00 and 9.30

am daily, would be shared equally, by running on alternate weeks, and both operators were warned of the consequences if they did not adhere to their conditions and timetables.

Nevertheless, the inevitable soon happened. On 29th June, 1927, the council's 'Watch Committee' reported that there were complaints of abusive conduct from the Ebsworth Bros. drivers, towards the rival service, and that they were running from Carmarthen, to the village of Llangunnock (Llangynog), which was not authorised. At the meeting, the licensing committee decided to revoke Ebsworth Bros.' three vehicle licences, and the authority to run Ebsworth Bros.' share of the Pendine to Carmarthen service, be given to Williams Bros.

A week later, the licensing committee held a special meeting, where Ebsworth Bros. gave an undertaking that they would comply with the committee's requirements, and were prepared to run their service to a timetable abandoned by Green's Motors, (Tenby to Carmarthen via Pendine), and stated they would comply with any other requirements. Two vehicle licences were reinstated with conditions, and a month later on 27th July, 1927, the third licence was reinstated to run between Carmarthen and Llangunnock.

Concurrently, on 29th June, 1927, a completely new operator, W. Evans, of 32 Meyrick Street, Pembroke Dock, asked for a licence to ply between Carmarthen and Pembroke Dock via Tenby. It was refused on the grounds that the route was adequately covered.

Above: A Dodge bus of Green's Motors, Haverfordwest, with re-issued registration number **DE 961,** is pictured here on the bus stand at Guildhall Square, Carmarthen, in 1925. It would have been working their twice daily service between Carmarthen and Pembroke Dock, via St Clears, Red Roses, Kilgetty, and Cross Inn. *(V. Morgan collection).*

The rivalry between Ebsworth Bros. and Williams Bros. nevertheless continued, and it was Williams Brothers' turn to have a warning from the Carmarthen B.C. licensing committee for irregular running on 27th July, 1927.

Nevertheless, a year later in June 1928, Tudor Williams Brothers asked the Carmarthen and Tenby B.C. licensing authorities, for a licence to operate a service linking the two towns, which was granted by both authorities a fortnight later in July 1928.

A month later, in August 1928, Ebsworth Bros. applied to the Tenby B.C., and asked the chief of police for support of their application, for two licences to ply within the Borough (*see letter opposite*). Surprisingly, they had not submitted an application for a Tenby to Carmarthen service. The licences they asked for were:-

[1] Tenby to Saundersfoot.

[2] Excursions from Tenby.

Both applications were immediately refused, in order to protect the services of a local operator, D.J. Morrison.

Concurrently, the Great Western Railway Co. were eager to expand their network of services, and applied to Carmarthen B.C. on 14th November, 1928, for three 'new' licences, Carmarthen to Pendine, Carmarthen to Pencader, and Carmarthen to Narberth. The licensing committee refused all three routes, as they were sufficiently covered by other operators. However, fifteen months later in February 1930, the Carmarthen to Narberth service, via St Clears and Whitland, was acquired by the reformed GWR Co. through their newly formed Western Welsh O.C. They acquired the route from the joint operators mentioned on page 13/14, Benjamin Davies of St Clears, and W. Edwards & Son of Towy Garage, Carmarthen.

Above: Two Ebsworth Bros. vehicles awaiting passengers at St Clears Railway Station, circa 1931. Nearest the camera is a Dodge, registered **BX 6628**, which was new to the company in March 1926. The driver, Georgie Jackson, is accompanied by passenger Miss Ali Beynon, and Arthur Leyshon Jenkins, driver of the company's 14 seat Chevrolet bus, **TH 617,** which was new in April 1930. Arthur started work with Ebsworth Bros. at the age of 14 in 1926, chauffeuring Miss Ali Beynon of Broadway, on a regular basis, and he remained faithfully with the company until its demise in 1954. The Chevrolet's body was advertised for sale, in 'as new condition', on 23rd May, 1933, when the vehicle was rebuilt as a lorry. *(Courtesy of Peter Jenkins).*

Above: Ebsworth Bros.' Lancia Pentaiota, **BX 7757**, with John Ebsworth, second from right, and Mervyn Roberts third from right. Mervyn became a shareholder and manager of the business, after its incorporation in 1944. *(Joan Griffiths).*

Above: This picture was not added to show off the ladies fashions for 1930, but to display the lettering on the rear end of the bus, 'Ebsworth Bros. <u>Laugharne and Pendine</u>'. The vehicle is thought to be Morris 'Viceroy', **TH 1725**.

Above: TH 618 was Ebsworth Bros.' first Leyland Tiger, and was delivered in May 1930, fitted with a locally built B32F body by Thomas & Thomas, Carmarthen. It was commandeered by the War Department for the RAF in July 1940, never to return, it was scrapped in February 1944. The vehicle behind was not owned by Ebsworth Bros, and is unidentified.   *(Roy Marshall)*.

Above: This Morris-Commercial 'Viceroy' YB6, **TH 1725**, delivered in May 1931, was also bodied by Thomas & Thomas, to B26D layout. It is photographed here working a private hiring, accompanied by Leyland TS4, TH 3333.   *(Roy Marshall)*.

In March 1930, Tudor Williams Brothers had their Carmarthen to Tenby licence revoked by Tenby B.C., having contravened their licence regulations – Neglecting their winter services amongst other compliances.

Ebsworth Bros. decided to apply for the Carmarthen to Tenby route, and submitted a licence application to both local authorities on 8th March, 1930, for a daily service to operate all year round between both towns. At the same time, they asked Tenby B.C. for two other licences to run daily services:-

[1] Tenby to Amroth via Kilgetty.   [2] Tenby to Clynderwen.

Three vehicle licences were issued, and the Carmarthen to Tenby licence was granted on 26th March, 1930, with an agreed timetable of one journey per day in each direction. The other two licence applications for Amroth and Clynderwen were refused on the grounds – they were protecting the services operated by D.J. Morrison of Tenby.

At the same meeting, Western Welsh were granted renewal of their Carmarthen – Narberth service with an extension to Tenby via Templeton, competing against Ebsworth Bros!

The following month, Tudor Williams Brothers gave an explanation to Tenby B.C. for the neglect of their winter service and other compliances, and proved that they were not picking up passengers on Morrison's route between Tenby and Begelly Cross. They succeeded in regaining their licence right away, but after several issues in May 1930, Ebsworth Bros. reported to Tenby B.C., that Williams Bros. had been running their Carmarthen to Tenby service on Ebsworth's times, and were not leaving Tenby in the evening in accordance with their timetable. Furthermore, they had not run their services at all on May 17/21/23/24/26th.

The council immediately decided to alter the evening scheduled times of both companies, and sent a warning letter to Williams Bros., stating 'You have not adhered to the timetable. If there are any more issues, we will deal severely with the matter'.

In July 1930, Ebsworth Bros. made another complaint to Tenby B.C. This time it was about the regulations stopping them from picking up passengers between Tenby and Begelly Cross, and on 1st August, 1930, Tenby B.C. sent notices to all operators *except* Tudor Williams Brothers, inviting them to renew their licences. Ebsworth Bros. received two vehicle licences, which were for BX 8540 & BX 9719.

In addition to all this, when the Road Traffic Act 1930 was implemented in April 1931, Tenby B.C. decided to oppose Williams Bros.' application for a Carmarthen to Tenby road service licence, provided that the opposing bus operators D.J. Morrison, and Ebsworth Bros., pay the council's expenses.

The arrangement was agreed upon by the opposing operators, resulting in the new licensing authority, the Ministry of Transport's Traffic Commissioners, rejecting Williams Bros.' renewal application for a road service licence between Carmarthen and Tenby.

Above: Ebsworth Bros. staff outing to Hereford in September 1937. The vehicle used was **TH 618**, a 1930 Leyland 'Tiger' TS2, with locally built bodywork by Thomas & Thomas of Carmarthen, to B32F layout. *(Courtesy of Peter Jenkins).*

Left: Another view of **TH 618**, the 1930 Leyland 'Tiger' TS2, which was captured at Guildhall Sq., Carmarthen, working a wintertime journey on the Carmarthen-Pendine service, which terminated at Laugharne.

The short gentleman on the left was a passenger, John Cheston from London, and the conductor, Arthur Jenkins (right), normally worked as a driver, but conducted for the company whenever required. He started working with Ebsworth Bros. at the age of 14, in 1926, and faithfully remained there until the company's demise in 1954. Guildhall Square was the terminus of their Carmarthen-Laugharne-Pendine service and the Carmarthen-Tenby service in those early days.

(Courtesy of Peter Jenkins).

EFFECTS OF THE ROAD TRAFFIC ACT 1930

The next major event in Ebsworth Bros.' history was The Road Traffic Act 1930. This Act of Parliament, which was passed in August 1930, gave the Ministry of Transport's Traffic Commissioners full control of public service vehicles (PSVs), together with passenger services and their licensing in Great Britain.

These Traffic Commissioners, with the power vested in them, brought about improved operating conditions, adherence to timetables, and stability of fares. All stage carriage and express service routes had to be licensed, and the granting of such licences, which had previously been under the jurisdiction of the local authorities, were then only obtainable through the Ministry of Transport's Traffic Commissioners. Licences to drive and conduct a PSV, also became the Traffic Commissioners responsibility. Under this new licensing system, all PSV operators were issued with operator identification numbers, by which they were identified. Consequently, the number issued to Ebsworth Brothers, of Fullerton House, King Street, Laugharne, was TGR 530, with each road service licence applied for thereafter, given licence application numbers beginning with the operator identification number.

After implementing the new Traffic Act fully in April 1931, every bus and coach operator had to re-apply to the new authority for renewal of each licence held, and re-apply annually thereafter. Likewise, any changes to services, times, fares, or new routes, all had to be applied for, and the licences would only be granted when approved by the Traffic Commissioners.

Conforming to the new licensing rules, Ebsworth Brothers applied for renewal without change, of all three stage carriage licences previously held by them. The following applications were published in the Traffic Commissioners first 'Notices & Proceedings' dated 25th March, 1931:-

TGR 530/1   **Carmarthen (Guildhall Square)** to **Tenby (South Parade)**.
via: Sarnau, St Clears, Red Roses, and Kilgetty.
To operate daily, including Sundays.

TGR 530/2   **Carmarthen (Guildhall Square)** to **Laugharne (The Grist)**.
via: Sarnau and St Clears, with an extension to Pendine, to run from June to October, and a Saturdays extension to Llangunnock (Llangynog).
To operate jointly with Williams Brothers daily, including Sundays.

TGR 530/3   **St Clears (Railway Station)** to **Laugharne (The Grist)**.
With extension to Pendine, from June to October.
To operate daily, including Sundays.

All three applications were objected to by competitors, Williams Bros., which led to a public hearing held at Shire Hall, Carmarthen, on 28th September, 1931. Licences TGR 530/1 and

530/2 were both granted on 29th September, 1931, but TGR 530/3 was refused on 21st October, 1931. Strangely, Ebsworth Bros. did not appeal against the decision.

However, when the annual licence renewals for TGR 530/1 and 530/2 came about in February 1932, Western Welsh objected to both applications, resulting in another public hearing on 5th October, 1932, where the licences were granted as before, with the same conditions applied to licence TGR 530/2: [1] The extension from Laugharne to Pendine shall be run daily in summer only, and on Saturdays only between 1st October and 31st May. [2] The licensee shall be entitled to run a duplicate bus from Laugharne into Carmarthen at 8 am, and a duplicate from Carmarthen at 9.00 pm and 11.00 pm on Wed/Sat only.

Consequently, Ebsworth Bros. and Williams Bros. retaliated against Western Welsh, and objected to their applications for Carmarthen to Tenby, TGR 441/46 and TGR 441/86, Narberth to Haverfordwest, resulting in an additional hearing at Shire Hall, Carmarthen, on the same occasion as TGR 530/1 and 530/2 above. WWOC received their renewals too!

On 6th July, 1932, Ebsworth Bros. applied to the Traffic Commissioners for through-booking facilities on their services TGR 530/1 and TGR 530/2. This facility was granted in January 1933 (see page 148 for fare table). At the same time, the company became a booking agent for Gough's Welsh Motorways' daily services, with interavailable through-bookings to most parts of South Wales, including Aberystwyth, Gloucester, Oxford, and London.

Above & Opposite: in addition to the buses, Ebsworth Bros. had a haulage business. They bought this very impressive Leyland 'Bull' TSQ3 side tipping lorry, registered **TH 2574** in June 1932, for a contract received at the Coygen Quarry, Laugharne. It was the first of four Leyland lorries acquired for the haulage fleet. *(Courtesy of The Leyland Society).*

Above: Another publicity photograph of the Leyland 'Bull', **TH 2574**, which is described opposite. *(The Leyland Society).*
Below: A working shot of **TH 2574** at Coygen Quarry, with John Ebsworth (*Jack*) standing in front. *(Courtesy of Joan Griffiths).*

The application mentioned above for through-booking facilities, was submitted jointly by Ebsworth Bros. and Gough's Welsh Motorways Ltd., of Mountain Ash, on 6th July, 1932, to use this combined fare table on Ebsworth Bros.' two services:-

TGR 530/1   [a] Carmarthen to Tenby, via Sarnau, St Clears, Red Roses and Kilgetty.
TGR 530/2   [b] Carmarthen to Pendine, via St Clears and Laugharne.

| | St Clears | | Laugharne | | Pendine | | Tenby | |
	S	R	S	R	S	R	S	R
Cardiff	8/3	11/5	8/9	12/3	9/6	13/3	10/3	13/9
Pontypridd	9/3	12/8	9/9	13/6	10/6	14/6	11/3	15/0
Abercynon	9/0	12/2	9/6	13/0	10/3	14/0	11/0	14/6
Mountain Ash	9/0	12/2	9/6	13/0	10/3	14/0	11/0	14/6
Aberdare	8/6	11/8	9/0	12/6	9/9	13/6	10/6	14/0
Porth	9/3	12/8	9/9	13/6	10/6	14/6	11/3	15/0
Tylorstown and Wattstown	9/0	12/5	9/6	13/3	10/3	14/3	11/0	14/9
Ferndale and Maerdy	9/0	12/2	9/6	13/0	10/3	14/0	11/0	14/6
Tonypandy and Penygraig	9/3	12/8	9/9	13/6	10/6	14/6	11/3	15/0
Treorchy, Pentre, Treherbert	9/0	12/2	9/6	13/0	10/3	14/0	11/0	14/6
Llantrisant (Talbot Green)	9/6	13/2	10/0	14/0	10/9	15/0	11/6	15/6
Tonyrefail	9/0	12/5	9/6	13/3	10/3	14/3	11/0	14/9
Glyn-Neath and Resolven	7/6	10/2	8/0	11/0	8/9	12/0	9/6	12/6
Aberdulais	6/9	9/2	7/3	10/0	8/0	11/0	8/9	11/6
Skewen	6/9	9/2	7/3	10/0	8/0	11/0	8/9	11/6
Aberayron	7/9	10/8	8/3	11/6	9/0	12/6	9/9	13/0
Aberystwyth	8/6	11/8	9/0	12/6	9/9	13/6	10/6	14/0
Cowbridge	8/3	11/2	8/9	12/0	9/6	13/0	10/3	13/6
Bridgend	7/9	10/8	8/3	11/6	9/0	12/6	9/9	13/0
Port Talbot	6/9	9/2	7/3	10/0	8/0	11/0	8/9	11/6
Neath	6/9	9/2	7/3	10/0	8/0	11/0	8/9	11/6
Llansamlet	6/9	9/2	7/3	10/0	8/0	11/0	8/9	11/6
Swansea	6/9	9/2	7/3	10/0	8/0	11/0	8/9	11/6
Gorseinon	6/9	9/2	7/3	10/0	8/0	11/0	8/9	11/6
Loughor	6/9	9/2	7/3	10/0	8/0	11/0	8/9	11/6
Llanelly	6/9	9/2	7/3	10/0	8/0	11/0	8/9	11/6

S = Single

R = Return

TELEGRAMS: EBSWORTH, LAUGHARNE
TELEPHONE: No. 11
STH. ST.-CLEARS

EBSWORTH BROTHERS

MOTOR PROPRIETORS

COACHES
CHARABANCS, CARS
AND LORRIES
FOR HIRE

FULLERTON HOUSE

ALSO STOCKISTS
TYRES, PETROL
OILS, ETC.

LAUGHARNE, CARMARTHEN

Ref............................   ....April....3rd.................1933.

Mr G. Meyrick Price.
Town Clerk.
Tenby.

      Dear Sir,

           We beg to acknowledge your letter of the
24th/ instant with/to the erection of a Bus Shelter at South Parade

           May we ask you how you propose to proportion the
cost to each Bus Proprietor , seeing that that the services are
not equal,and that,all the Bus Proprietors have not the same interests
in such proposal.

           If you will kindly give us an approx idea we will
then give the matter our serious consideration.

           Thanking you.

                Yours faithfully.
                 PER. PRO:
                   EBSWORTH BROS.
                      J. L. Ebsworth.

Above: This letter was written on 3rd April, 1933, by John Lewis Ebsworth (Jack Ebsworth), manager of Ebsworth Bros., and was sent to the clerk of Tenby B.C., expressing his concerns over the shared costs of erecting a bus shelter at South Parade, Tenby. The planned bus shelters in South Parade never materialised. *(CBPG Archive).*

Ebsworth Brothers' Summer Time Table

CARMARTHEN, ST. CLEARS, TENBY, LAUGHARNE and PENDINE

CARMARTHEN, ST. CLEARS, LAUGHARNE & PENDINE.

	a.m.	p.m.	p.m.	p.m.	p.m.	p.m.	p.m.	p.m.	p.m.
Carmarthen .....dep.	9.0	11.0	X1.0	3.0	5.0	7.0	9.0	11.0	P11.0
Pass - By	9.15	11.15	1.15	3.15	5.15	7.15	9.15	11.15	P11.15
Bankyfelin	9.20	11.20	1.20	3.20	5.20	7.20	9.20	11.20	P11.20
St. Clears	9.27	11.27	1.27	3.27	5.27	7.27	9.27	11.27	P11.27
Laugharne ....arr.	9.40	11.40	1.40	3.40	5.40	7.40	9.40	11.40	P11.40
Pendine ......arr.	9.55	11.55	1.55	—	5.55	7.55			

	a.m.	p.m.	p.m.	p.m.	p.m.	p.m.	p.m.
Pendine .....dept.		10.0	12.0	*2.0	—	6.0	8.0
Laugharne	8.0	10.15	12.15	2.15	4.15	6.15	8.15
St. Clears	8.15	10.25	12.25	2.25	4.25	6.25	8.25
Bankyfelin	8.25	10.2?	12.35	2.35	4.35	6.35	8.35
Pass - By	8.30	10.40	12.45	2.40	4.40	6.40	8.40
Carmarthen	8.45	10.55	12.55	2.55	4.55	6.40	8.55

X—Thursday, 1.15 p.m. P—(Or after Pictures) *On Thursday at 4 p.m. instead.

CARMARTHEN, ST. CLEARS, TENBY.

	a.m.	p.m.	p.m.
Carmarthen dept.	9.0	11.0	X1.0
Laugharne dept.	9.15	11.15	1.15
St. Clears	9.27	11.27	1.27
Llanddowror	9.35	11.35	1.35
Red Roses	9.45	11.45	1.45
Llanteg	9.50	11.50	1.50
Commercial	10.0	*12.0	2.0
Kilgetty	10.8	*12.8	2.8
Tenby ...... arr.	10.25	*12.25	2.25

	p.m.	a.m.	p.m.	p.m.	p.m.
Tenby ...... dept.	5.0	11.35	*1.35	3.35	7.35
Kilgetty	5.27	11.52	*1.52	3.52	7.52
Commercial	5.35	12.0	*2.0	4.0	8.0
Llanteg	5.35	12.5	*2.5	4.5	8.5
Red Roses	5.45	12.10	*2.10	4.10	8.10
Llanddowror	5.50	12.20	*2.20	4.20	8.20
St. Clears	6.0	12.25	*2.25	4.25	8.25
Laugharne	6.8	12.40	*2.40	4.40	8.40
Carmarthen arr.	6.25	12.55	*2.55	4.55	8.55

X—Thursday 1-15 p.m. *—Run during Aug. only.

SUNDAY SERVICES.

	p.m.	p.m.	p.m.
Carmarthen dept	1.15	7.0	9.0
Pass By	1.30	7.15	9.15
Bankyfelin	1.35	7.20	9.20
St. Clears	1.45	7.27	9.30
Laugharne arr.	2.0	7.40	9.45
Pendine arr.	2.15	7.55	

	p.m.	p.m.	p.m.
Pendine Dept. ...	—	6.0	8.0
Laugharne	1.30	6.15	8.15
St. Clears	1.45	6.25	8.25
Bankyfelin	—	6.35	8.35
Pass - By	—	6.40	8.40
Carmarthen Arr	12.55	6.55	8.55

SUNDAY SERVICES.

	p.m.
Carmarthen dept.	1.15
St. Clears	1.45
Llanddowror	1.50
Red Roses	2.0
Llanteg	2.5
Commercial	2.10
Kilgetty	2.23
Tenby arr.	2.40

	p.m.
Tenby Dept.	7.35
Kilgetty	7.52
Commercial	8.0
Llanteg	8.5
Red Roses	8.10
Llanddowror	8.20
St. Clears	8.25
Carmarthen Arr.	8.55

IMPORTANT NOTICES - - STOPS.—Passengers are respectfully requested to give a clear and distinct signal by raising the hand when wishing a bus to stop on the road. Passengers will greatly assist in stopping our buses only at the recognised stops as far as possible. 2.—Passengers MUST receive the proper priced ticket for the fare paid PUNCHED IN THEIR PRESENCE. 3.—RETURN Tickets are available for the Return Journey for an indefinite period. 4.—TIMES ARE APPROXIMATE. In the case of frost, snow, fog or other exceptional conditions of the road it may be necessary to curtail or discontinue Services without notice, and no liability can be accepted for inconvenience caused. 5.—All reasonable care will be taken to ensure that our buses make connections with our different routes, and those of other bus proprietors, but no connection is guaranteed, neither do we accept liability for any inconvenience caused through failing to do so.

PARCELS CAN BE SENT BY ALL OUR BUSES. These must be PREPAID and are only accepted and conveyed at OWNERS' RISK.

EBSWORTH BROS., LAUGHARNE   'Phone: 11.

"Cymric Times," Ltd., Carmarthen

Above: Ebsworth Bros.' staff looked very professional in their uniforms during the 1930s. This view of **TH 3333**, a 1933 Leyland 'Tiger' TS4, with Thomas & Thomas bodywork built to B35D layout, was taken at St Clears. The vehicle was working the Carmarthen to Tenby service, but the crew awaited a scheduled connection here at St Clears, for transfer of passengers off the service from Pendine.
(Courtesy of Peter Jenkins).

Left: This view of Leyland 'Tiger' **TH 3333**, was taken outside St Clears Market with conductor, Arthur Jenkins, posing in front of the bus. Arthur was normally a driver, but on this occasion was conducting the bus.
TH 3333 was new to Ebsworth Bros. in April 1933.
(Photo courtesy of Peter Jenkins, Arthur Jenkins' son).

The next licence applications came two months later on 13th September, 1933:-

TGR 530/4   **Excursions & Tours**
Starting from: [1] The Garage, King St., Laugharne.
[2] Beach Hotel, Pendine.
[3] Blue Boar Square, Carmarthen Rd, St Clears.
Tours will run throughout the year.

The above licence was granted on 4th October, 1933, and by December 1934, it had been changed to Excursions & Tours starting from 'The Garage, King St., Laugharne', only.

TGR 530/Sp/1   Was issued to operate an excursion from St Clears to Mydrim on 27/9/1933 only.

On 4th October, 1933, the Traffic Commissioner, Mr A.T. James (KC) (chairman), Alderman James of Caerphilly, and Councillor H.S. Holmes of Carmarthen, met at Carmarthen's Guildhall to make an annual review of motor bus services in the area.

One item on the agenda, was an issue reported by Ebsworth Bros., regarding Tudor Williams Brothers not running in accordance with their timetable, and charging fares at less than the recognised amount on the Carmarthen - Pendine service. It was also stated that there was an agreed timetable, fare table, and interavailability of return tickets between them.

Mr A.T. James (KC), reprimanded Tudor Williams in court, and decided to suspend Williams Bros.' licences for 4 weeks, from Monday 9th October to Sunday 5th November, 1933, inclusive, and arranged that during the suspension period, Western Welsh O.C. would run the journeys authorised to Williams Bros. on the jointly operated service, in order not to inconvenience the public.

Ebsworth Bros. applied for two more licences on 9th May, 1934, which are listed below:-

TGR 530/5   **Excursions & Tours**, starting from St Clears.

TGR 530/6   **Excursions & Tours**, starting from Carmarthen.

An objection to TGR 530/5 was received from Great Western Railway (Railway Executive). The licence was granted on 24th October, 1934.

Objectors to TGR 530/6 were Great Western Railway (Railway Executive); LMS Railway; The South Wales Transport Company, Swansea; and Tudor Williams Bros., Laugharne. The licence was granted on 24th October, 1934, with the same special conditions as applied to Tudor Williams Bros.' licence TGR 457/9.

In the meantime however, negotiations had taken place on 10th July, 1934, regarding the sale of Ebsworth Bros.' bus business to Western Welsh O.C. Their offer of £4,000 was rejected.

Western Welsh returned with a new offer of 'under £5,000' on 18th September, 1934, which was considered. The offer included the purchase of their entire PSV fleet, 3 Leylands, 1 Morris, and 1 Chevrolet bus, valued at £2,180, subject to verification of mileage receipts.

The deal fell through on 22nd November, 1934, as they were unable to substantiate mileage and receipts.

The following day, 23rd November, 1934, negotiations began with Bassett's of Gorseinon, but those negotiations fell through too!

It appears that by this point in time, the brothers were concentrating more on the haulage side of their business, as there were three more Leyland lorries added to the haulage fleet. TH 2901, in November 1932, TH 4908 in November 1934, and TH 7062 in May 1936, and in 1938, further additions were made to the haulage fleet, with no less than six Internationals.

In comparison, the bus fleet received one Leyland 'Tiger' TS7, TH 5515, in June 1935, and the first double-decker in their fleet, TH 9010, a Leyland TD5 'Titan', in July 1937.

Above: The first double-decker vehicle in the fleet, **TH 9010**, was this Leyland 'Titan' TD7 with Leyland L27/26R bodywork, which was purchased new by the company in July 1937. This vehicle would have been used on the Carmarthen - Tenby route *after* WW2, due to the high demand in summertime. However, it was vital to employ 'lowbridge' type deckers on that service, as there were low bridges at Kilgetty, and Moreton. **TH 9010** is pictured opposite Ebsworth Bros.' first garage in King Street, Laugharne, with Fullerton House, the company's office on the right. Fullerton House doubled as the company's office, and home to John Ebsworth's family and his brother Thomas Ebsworth's family, until 1937, when control of the bus business passed entirely to Tom, a former Grenadier Guards Lieutenant. Tom sadly passed away in January 1942, at the age of 53.

(V. Morgan collection).

Left: This view of Leyland 'Titan' **TH 9010** was taken at Western Welsh' graveyard at Ely Works, Cardiff, in 1955, after the Ebsworth Bros. takeover, December 1954. It was not operated by Western Welsh, even though it was allocated fleet number 984. It was eventually sold for scrap in June 1956.

The vehicle on the right is a former James of Ammanford, Daimler CWA6, CBX 299, which also awaited disposal. The complete history of J. James & Sons, Ammanford is currently still available at: vernonmorgan.com

(Roy Marshall).

Above: **ABX 467** was a Bedford WTB with Duple C26F bodywork, which was purchased new in July 1938. It is accompanied by **ETH 785**, a Crossley SD42/7, new to Ebsworth Bros. in April 1949, with C33F coachwork built by D.J. Davies of Treforest. This view was taken in 1950, inside the company's new depot, Clifton Garage, Laugharne, which had been converted from an old timber yard, shortly before the outbreak of World War 2. *(Alan Cross).*

Above: Another view of **ABX 467**, the company's 1938 Bedford WTB, with Duple 26 seat body, which is seen working a private charter. When this vehicle came off passenger service in November 1950, driver Arthur Jenkins bought it, and with assistance from his brother, converted it into a mobile Fish & Chip shop, which became a regular visitor to Pendine Sands. A picture of this vehicle in its new guise can be seen on page 189. *(Courtesy of 'Chips' Peter Jenkins).*

Above: King Street, Laugharne, in 1938, depicting Brown's Hotel (right) with Fullerton House next door. Brown's Hotel Garage, which Ebsworth Bros. leased and renamed Central Garage, is seen on the left with the 'Shell' sign. In April 1937, Tudor Williams' brother, Ebie, purchased Brown's Hotel and its garage, resulting in Ebsworth Bros. quickly vacating the property.

As mentioned earlier, the company rented 'Central Garage' in King Street, Laugharne, from the Brown's Hotel, but it was hastily vacated in April 1937, after Tudor Williams' younger brother Ebie, acquired it with the purchase of the Brown's Hotel.

The Ebsworth brothers quickly bought an old Timber Yard, and a garden previously owned by the Broadway Estate, some 400 metres away from Central Garage, in Clifton Street, which was cleared to build a garage, named Clifton Garage. At the same time, John Ebsworth moved house to live closer to the new garage, and bought Clifton House, in Clifton Street. His brother Tom remained at Fullerton House, and took over as manager of the bus business.

Nevertheless, it was commonly known that Western Welsh and Ebsworth Bros. were rivals too, but in February 1938, an amicable arrangement was formed between them. Western Welsh applied to the Traffic Commissioners on 16th February, 1938, for permission to allow through-bookings on their Cardiff to Carmarthen service, in conjunction with the services of Ebsworth Bros. from Carmarthen to St Clears, Laugharne, Pendine and Tenby, on a summation basis, by adding certain amounts to fares.

Additionally, interavailability of return and weekly tickets was authorised between Ebsworth Bros. and D.J. Morrison, Tenby, in August 1938, on the section of Ebsworth Bros.' Carmarthen to Tenby service, between Kilgetty and Tenby.

A year later, when World War 2 began in September 1939, the company were compelled to introduce emergency timetables in order to conserve fuel and rubber. Services were reduced to a very basic frequency, simply a service accommodating workers.

Ten months later in July 1940, War Department Officials toured all bus and coach operators in the UK, requisitioning buses and coaches for military use, usually taking the operators best buses and coaches. In Ebsworth Brothers' case, two elderly Leyland saloons were requisitioned, and never returned.

Work during the war years became exceptionally quiet for the passenger sector of the business due to the government restrictions, but authorisation was sanctioned by the Ministry of War Transport for the purchase of one second hand double-decker in November 1942, which replaced the two Leyland saloons requisition in 1940.

Unfortunately, Tom Ebsworth's wife, Rose Emily, passed away in December 1941, and after a brief illness, Tom sadly passed away 5 weeks later, having suffered a heart attack on 31st January, 1942.

This came as a great shock to everyone involved in the business, and to all his friends within the neighbourhood, which had become his home.

An emotional tribute to Tom Ebsworth, was published in a local newspaper immediately after his death, which read:-

'Death of Captain Thomas Lewis Ebsworth'.

'We regret to announce the death of Captain Thomas Lewis Ebsworth, of Fullerton House, Laugharne, which occurred on Sunday morning after a brief illness.

He was a senior partner in the firm of Ebsworth Brothers, motor bus and garage proprietors, and haulage contractors, Clifton Garage, Laugharne.

Mr. Ebsworth established the business in a small way in 1919, in partnership with his brother John Ebsworth, when they came from Pendine, and took up residence in Laugharne.

Deceased entered wholeheartedly into the life of the town, taking an active interest in all local affairs, becoming a Burgess of the Corporation, and served for a period as foreman of the grand jury.

He was a member and past chairman of the Township Parish Council, and an active member of the Sports Committee, and Regatta committee, of which he was vice president.

A staunch supporter of the Billiard Room and Social club, Mr. Ebsworth was noted for his generosity and willingness to support every worthy cause.

He was the junior trustee of the Abercorran Lodge of Oddfellows, and a Brother of the Narberth branch of Freemason's, in which he took an active interest, having carried out the duties of Secretary for some time. He held provincial honours, and was Past Master.

In his younger days, Mr. Ebsworth served for a period in the Welsh Guards, and at the outbreak of war in 1914, enlisted in the 8th Welsh, in the ranks. He served in France throughout the campaign, with distinction, being awarded 'Croix de Guerre' by the French Government, for distinguished bravery in a field. He was soon given a commission.

Since the establishment of the Home Guard, he had taken an active part in the raising of the local company, of which he was Captain. On medical advice, he had to relinquish his command a few weeks ago, which was a source of great regret to him.

His death is all the more tragic, because of the loss of his wife only five weeks ago.

They leave an only son, Thomas Ebsworth, to mourn his loss, and with whom much sympathy is extended.

The funeral and burial took place at St Martin's Church, Laugharne yesterday.'

Dated 4th February, 1942.

Notes: Tom Ebsworth had received the title of 'Captain' at the Home Guard.

Abercorran, is the original name for Laugharne Castle.

After Tom's death, his brother John took the helm once again, this time from his new home, Clifton House, in Clifton Street. Soon afterwards he moved house again to live in Tenby, running both transport concerns from his home at Narberth Road in Tenby. His brother David, who was still running the Beach Hotel in Pendine, then took up residence in Clifton House, to manage Clifton Garage. He remained at Clifton House until his death in February 1956, when his status was given as 'garage proprietor'.

The only passenger vehicle acquired by the company during WW2, was WJ 9093, a former Sheffield Corporation (fleet no. A93), Leyland 'Titan' TD3, with bodywork built by Cravens Railway Carriage & Wagon Co. of Sheffield. This vehicle, which arrived in November 1942, was a replacement for the two Leyland saloons commandeered by the Ministry of War Transport in July 1940.

Above: The only vehicle acquired during WW2 was **WJ 9093**, a 1934, former Sheffield Corporation (A93), Leyland 'Titan' TD3c, (converted to diesel engine and manual gearbox) with a H31/24R body built by Cravens Railway Carriage and Wagon Co. of Sheffield. It arrived at Laugharne, via Walter Alexander, Falkirk, (R324, not operated), in November 1942, with full approval of the Ministry of War Transport. This was a replacement for two Leyland saloons commandeered by the MOWT in 1940, and is pictured inside Clifton Garage, Laugharne, in 1950. It's accompanied by former Premier Omnibus Co., London, re-bodied Leyland 'Titan' TD1, **GJ 7537**, details of which are on page 161. *(Alan Cross)*

EBSWORTH BROTHERS' INCORPORATION

After the untimely death of Thomas Ebsworth in January 1942, the remaining partnership decided to register the omnibus business as a limited company, and on 22nd August, 1944, the company was incorporated as **Ebsworth Brothers Ltd.**, with registered number 0389376. The directors were given as John Lewis Ebsworth, bus proprietor, of Clifton House, Laugharne, and his wife, Lilian Edna Ebsworth, secretary, Clifton House, Laugharne. Arrangements were made by Julian S. Hodge & Co., 31 Windsor Place, Cardiff.

In March 1945, Julian Stephen Hodge, of Bryn Road, Pontllanfraith (financier) and William Mervyn Roberts of Victoria Street, Laugharne (Ebsworth Bros.' garage foreman), became shareholders, and in May 1945, the company's registered address was changed from Clifton Garage, Laugharne, to 31 Windsor Place, Cardiff. At the same time, Justin Rowland Jenkins, of Cross Keys, Monmouthshire, became a director. Jenkins was also a director of Bryn Motor Co., Pontllanfraith, another bus company, and in subsequent years, shareholders and directors interchanged quite regularly.

After registration of the limited company, two years had lapsed before management applied to the Traffic Commissioners for transferral of the licences held by the original licence holder, 'Ebsworth Brothers'. This legal requirement of notifying change of entity to a Limited company, had not been carried out due to the fact that licensing issues were still being maintained by the Ministry of War Transport. The renewals were finally applied for on 23rd October, 1946, as follows:-

TGR 3563/1   Previously   TGR 530/1   **Carmarthen** to **Tenby** (**South Parade**), via: Sarnau, St Clears, Llanddowror and Kilgetty.

TGR 3563/2   "   TGR 530/2   **Carmarthen** to **Pendine**, via Laugharne.

Also applied for on 23rd October, 1946 was a licence in respect of a service introduced subsequent to 3rd September, 1939, to provide a stage carriage service between Pendine and Tenby (South Parade) via Laugharne, St Clears, Llanddowror and Kilgetty. Daily throughout the year, Sundays during summer only. *This application was given an out of sequence number:-* TGR 3563/6.

D.J. Morrison, Tenby, objected to applications TGR 3563/1 and 3563/6, on 20th November, 1946, but they were granted together with TGR 3563/2, on 8th January, 1947.

An additional three licence renewals were applied for on 22nd January, 1947:-

TGR 3563/3   Previously   TGR 530/4   **Excursions & Tours** starting from Laugharne.

TGR 3563/4   "   TGR 530/3   **Excursions & Tours** starting from St Clears, (Blue Boar or Corvus Terrace).

EBSWORTH BROTHERS LTD.

TIME TABLE

Passenger Service throughout the Year

CARMARTHEN - TENBY - PENDINE

PENDINE : LAUGHARNE : ST. CLEARS : CARMARTHEN

WEEK-DAYS		a.m.	a.m.	a.m.	p.m.	p.m.	p.m.	p.m.	p.m.	p.m.
Pendine	Dept.	7.45	10.00	12.00	2.00	4.00	6.00	8.00	10.00	12.00
Laugharne	...	8.00	10.15	12.15	2.15	4.15	6.15	8.15	10.15	12.15
St. Clears	...	8.15	10.25	12.25	2.25	4.25	6.25	8.25	10.25	
Bancyfelin	...	8.25	10.35	12.35	2.35	4.35	6.35	8.35	10.35	
Pass-By	...	8.30	10.40	12.40	2.40	4.40	6.40	8.40	10.40	
Carmarthen	arr.	8.45	10.55	12.55	2.55	4.55	6.55	8.55	10.55	

		a.m.	a.m.	p.m.	p.m.	p.m.	p.m.	p.m.	p.m.	p.m.
Carmarthen	Dept.	9.00	11.00	1.00	3.00	5.00	7.00	9.00	11.00	
Pass-By	...	9.15	11.15	1.15	3.15	5.15	7.15	9.15	11.15	
Bancyfelin	...	9.20	11.20	1.20	3.20	5.20	7.20	9.20	11.20	
St. Clears	...	9.25	11.25	1.25	3.25	5.25	7.25	9.25	11.25	
Laugharne	...	9.40	11.40	1.40	3.40	5.40	7.40	9.40	11.40	
Pendine	arr.	9.55	11.55	1.55	3.55	5.55	7.55	9.55	11.55	

PENDINE : LAUGHARNE : ST. CLEARS : TENBY

WEEK-DAYS		a.m.	a.m.	a.m.	p.m.	p.m.
Pendine	Dept.		9.00	12.00	4.00	8.00
Laugharne	...		9.15	12.15	4.15	8.15
St. Clears	...		9.25	12.25	4.25	8.25
Tenby	arr.		10.25	1.25	5.25	9.25
Tenby	Dept.		10.30	2.30	6.30	9.30
St. Clears	...		11.30	3.30	7.30	10.30
Laugharne	...	8.40	11.40	3.40	7.40	10.40
Pendine	arr.	8.55	11.55	3.55	7.55	

CARMARTHEN : ST. CLEARS : KILGETTY : TENBY

WEEK-DAYS.		a.m.	p.m.	p.m.	p.m.
Carmarthen	Dept.	9.00	12.05*	4.05*	8.05*
St. Clears	...	9.30	12.30*	4.30*	8.30*
Llanddowror	...	9.35	12.35	4.35	8.35
Red Roses	...	9.45	12.45	4.45	8.45
Llanteg	...	9.50	12.50	4.50	8.50
Commercial	...	10.00	1.00	5.00	9.00
Kilgetty	...	10.08	1.08	5.08	9.08
Tenby	arr.	10.25	1.25	5.25	9.25
Tenby	Dept.	10.30	2.30	6.30	9.30
Kilgetty	...	10.47	2.47	6.47	9.47
Commercial	...	10.55	2.55	6.55	9.55
Llanteg	...	11.00	3.00	7.00	10.00
Red Roses	...	11.05	3.05	7.05	10.05
Llanddowror	...	11.15	3.15	7.15	10.15
St. Clears	...	11.30*	3.30*	7.30*	10.30
Carmarthen	arr.	11.55*	3.55*	7.55*	10.55

* On these journeys no passengers will be picked up or set down at any point between St. Clears or Carmarthen or between Carmarthen and St. Clears except for points beyond St. Clears.

S.Ld.—56te.

Above: This was Ebsworth Bros' weekday timetable for TGR 3563/2, 3563/6, 3563/1, respectively, dated October 1946.

Above: This Leyland 'Titan' TD1, **GJ 7537**, (which also appears on page 158), was acquired in May 1946, and had a very interesting history. It was new to Premier Omnibus Co., London, in June 1930 (pictured below), with a Duple body. It passed to London PTB in December 1933, and later to Valliant, Hendon. In 1945, it was re-bodied with this Burlingham H29/26R body, for Green, Brierly Hill, West Midlands. Ebsworth Bros. bought it May 1946, and sold it to Williams Bros. Laugharne in 1951, passing to Lansdowne, London E11, in May 1955, where this view was taken.   *(Both views courtesy of The Bus Archive).*
Below: This is a view of **GJ 7537** in its original guise, bodied by Duple with an open cab and staircase. See all details above.

Above: A splendid shot of Ebsworth Bros.' Leyland 'Titan' PD1, **CTH 828**, with Leyland L27/26R body, pictured on the old A40 trunk road (Pentre Road, St Clears), on a journey into Carmarthen. The Milford Arms in the background was later renamed 'The Highwayman', but is nowadays, the St Clears Pharmacy. This location in Pentre Road, is the junction with Station Road, B4299 to Mydrim – note the 'finger-post' road sign. *(The Bus Archive)*.

The following new licence application was made on 22nd January, 1947:-

TGR 3563/7   **Excursions & Tours** starting from Pendine, with picking up points at Laugharne, St Clears, and Carmarthen.

All four licence applications, TGR 3563/3, 4, 5, and 7, were granted on 16th April, 1947.

And in February 1947, two workmen's stage carriage services were applied for:-

TGR 3563/8   **St Clears** to **Pendine (Ministry of Supply Experimental Establishment)** picking up at intermediate stages as required – Cross Inn, Laugharne, Broadway, and Brook.   *Monday to Friday only.* *Fares deducted from wages at source.*

TGR 3563/9   **Laugharne** to **Pendine (M o S Experimental Establishment)** via: Broadway, Brook, Llanmilo and Central Site. *Monday to Friday only. Fares: Laugharne (The Grist) to Pendine MoS, 3/- weekly or 7d return daily, deducted from wages by M o S.*

The above two applications TGR 3563/8, and 9, were granted on 9th July, 1947.

Above: **BDW 13** was a Leyland 'Tiger' TS8, with Weymann B36F body, which was new to Newport Corporation in August 1937, with dual entrance, B33D. It was purchased in 1948, from Corvedale Motors, Ludlow, Shropshire (f/n15). *(Alan Cross)*.

Above: This Crossley SD42/7, **ETH 785,** with C33F coachwork by D.J. Davies, Treforest, was delivered in April 1949. It was transferred to associate company, Jeremy's Garages, Tenby, in June 1952, but returned unused in October 1953, after failing to obtain an operators licence. Alongside is former Newport, Leyland 'Tiger' TS8, BDW 13. *(Courtesy of James & Joan Griffiths)*.

Above: **FBX 35** was the only Dennis chassis acquired by Ebsworth Bros. This Dennis 'Lance III', with H30/26R bodywork, built by D.J. Davies of Treforest, was new to the company in June 1949. It was identical to the one delivered to competitors, Williams Brothers six months earlier, and had consecutive chassis numbers. **FBX 35** is pictured here at Lammas Street, Carmarthen, accompanied by Ebsworth Bros.' Leyland PD2, FTH 445.

(V. Morgan collection).

Left: This is another shot of the Dennis 'Lance III', **FBX 35**, working the Pendine service in 1950. It could not operate the Tenby service due to low bridges situated along the route, so was a regular performer of the Carmarthen – Pendine service.

(Alan Cross).

Above: This advertisement for D.J. Davies' coachbuilding activities, features a Dennis 'Lance III' similar to the ones delivered to Ebsworth Bros. and Williams Bros. in 1949. It will be noticed, however, that D.J. Davies also traded as Wheatsheaf Motors, a PSV operator at Merthyr Tydfil. *(The Bus Archive).*

Another workmen's Express Carriage licence was applied for on 31st August, 1949:-

TGR 3563/10   **Carmarthen** to **Pendine** (**MoS Experimental Establishment**). via: Bankyfelin, St Clears, and Laugharne.

This was issued on 21st December, 1949, with the same condition as applied to Williams Bros.' licence TGR 457/12:- The PSVs used on the authorised service are to be garaged in Carmarthen from Monday to Friday inclusive of each week, during which the service is to be operated. On 30th August, 1950, Ebsworth Bros. asked for the above condition to be deleted from the licence, and it was granted on 22nd November, 1950.

Meanwhile, on 26th October, 1949, a modification was asked for on their stage carriage service licence TGR 3563/1, Carmarthen to Tenby. The modification, to use double decker buses on the route (lowbridge type only), was granted on 21st December, 1949.

TGR 3563/2: The Sats only extension to Llangunnock, was discontinued by October 1946.

DISTINGUISHED COACHWORK

BY

=== D. J. DAVIES ===

Illustration shows the DAVIES 1949 Model LUXURY COACH Body mounted on a LEYLAND PSI chassis.

Luxuriously appointed 33 seater fitted with the latest built-in heater, air conditioning, and Radiomobile wireless equipment.

Write or phone now for full specification and delivery.

Single and Double Deck bodies constructed on all makes of chassis.

D. J. DAVIES
TREFOREST TRADING ESTATE

PHONE: TAFFS WELL 290 (3 LINES)   GLAM.

Above: This D.J. Davies advertisement depicts Ebsworth Bros.' 1949 Leyland PS1, **FBX 491**. *(Courtesy of The Bus Archive).*

Above: A splendid publicity shot of Ebsworth Bros.' **FBX 491**, a Leyland 'Tiger' PS1/1, with D.J. Davies C33F coachwork, which was photographed at Cyfarthfa Castle, Merthyr Tydfil, in 1949.   *(Courtesy of The Bus Archive).*

Above: Another example of D.J. Davies' coachwork, was fitted to Ebsworth Bros.' Leyland PS1/1, **FBX 754**, which differed from FBX 491 above, by way of a canopy, ventilated windows, and bus seating for 35 passengers built to dual purpose standards. This view was taken outside B.T. Jones, coal merchants office, Lammas St, Carmarthen.   *(Dr Michael A. Taylor).*

Above: A front n/s view of Leyland 'Tiger' **FBX 754**, loading up for Carmarthen, inside Clifton Garage in 1950. *(Alan Cross).*

Above: This Leyland 'Titan' PD2/1, **FTH 445,** with Leyland L27/26R low-bridge body, was ordered by Ebsworth Bros. after they received permission from the Traffic Commissioners to use double deckers on the Carmarthen - Tenby service in December 1949. It arrived in June 1950, and is pictured here on lay-over, outside St John's Church, Warren Street, Tenby, with the town wall in the backdrop. It was awaiting departure time from South Parade, for the return trip to Carmarthen. *(Dr Michael Taylor).*

In June 1950, competitors Williams Bros. got themselves into deep trouble with the Traffic Commissioners, over an issue regarding wages and under paying their staff. It was stated that the rate of wages and conditions of employment were less than favourable.

The South Wales Traffic Commissioners gave notice of their proposals to revoke Williams Bros.' licence if the matter was not settled, and four weeks later on 11th October, 1950, the notice was cancelled.

Details of this can be found on pages 38/39.

As a direct result of this incident, Williams Bros. and Ebsworth Bros. collaborated and asked the Traffic commissioners for permission to revise fares on their jointly operated Carmarthen - Pendine services, TGR 3563/2 and TGR 457/2 respectively.

The proposed fare table dated 3rd January, 1951, is reproduced below:-

```
Carmarthen.
2d.   Johnstown.
4d.   3d.   Travellers' Rest.
5d.   4d.   3d.   Maesyprior.
6d.   5d.   4d.   3d.   Pass Bye.
8d.   6d.   5d.   4d.   3d.   Sarnau Road.
9d.   7d.   6d.   5d.   4d.   3d.   Bankyfelin.
10d.  8d.   7d. , 6d.   5d.   4d.   3d.   Rushmoor.
11d.  9d.   8d.   7d.   6d.   5d.   4d.   3d.   New Church.
1/1   11d.  10d.  9d.   8d.   7d.   6d.   5d.   3d.   Upper St. Clears.
1/3   1/1   1/-   11d.  10d.  8d.   7d.   6d.   5d.   3d.   Lower St. Clears.
1/4   1/2   1/1   1/-   11d.  9d.   8d.   7d.   6d.   5d.   3d.   Morfa Bach.
1/5   1/3   1/2   1/1   1/-   10d.  9d.   8d.   7d.   6d.   5d.   3d.   Cross Inn.
1/7   1/5   1/4   1/3   1/2   1/-   11d.  10d.  9d.   8d.   7d.   5d.   3d.   Laugharne.
1/9   1/7   1/6   1/5   1/4   1/2   1/1   1/-   11d.  9d.   8d.   7d.   6d.   Mansion.
1/11  1/9   1/8   1/7   1/6   1/4   1/3   1/2   1/1   11d.  9d.   8d.   7d.   Plashett.
2/1   1/11  1/10  1/9   1/8   1/6   1/5   1/4   1/3   1/1   11d.  10d.  9d.   Brook.
2/2   2/1   1/11  1/10  1/9   1/7   1/6   1/5   1/4   1/2   1/-   11d.  10d.  Llanmiloe.
2/3   2/2   2/1   2/-   1/11  1/9   1/8   1/7   1/6   1/4   1/2   1/1   1/-   Pendine.

Laugharne.
4d.   Mansion.
5d.   3d.   Plashett.
6d.   4d.   3d.   Brook.
8d.   6d.   5d.   4d.   Llanmiloe.
9d.   8d.   7d.   6d.   3d.   Pendine.

Special Return : Laugharne—Pendine  ..  1/3.

Children over 3 and under 14 years of age, half-fare. with
      minimum fare of 1d.
```

```
Ordinary Returns :—
      S.    R.          S.    R.
4d.   ..   7d.         1/4   ..   2/3
5d.   ..   9d.         1/5   ..   2/5
6d.   ..   10d.        1/7   ..   2/8
7d.   ..   1/-         1/9   ..   3/-
8d.   ..   1/3         1/11  ..   3/2
9d.   ..   1/5         2/1   ..   3/5
11d.  ..   1/7         2/2   ..   3/6
1/1   ..   1/9         2/3   ..   3/8
1/3   ..   2/-         2/6   ..   4/-
```

This fare table was withdrawn six weeks later and substituted with a new revised fare table asking for an increase of 25%, which was granted to both operators on 23rd May, 1951.

Additionally, on 17th January, 1951, Ebsworth Bros. asked for fare increases on their Carmarthen to Tenby service TGR 3563/1, and Pendine to Tenby service, TGR 3563/6. Both applications were withdrawn on 14th February, submitting new applications with larger increases two weeks later on 28th February, which were granted on 23rd May, 1951.

The fare tables mentioned on the previous page, for services TGR 3563/1 and TGR 3563/6, are reproduced below and opposite:-

Ebsworth Bros., Ltd., of Clifton Garage, Laugharne. Stage carriages :—
3563/1—Between Carmarthen and Tenby. Revised fare table :—

```
Carmarthen.
S. .. 2d.  Johnstown.
S. .. 4d.  3d.  Travellers Rest.
S. .. 5d.  4d.  3d.  Maesyprior.
S. .. 6d.  5d.  4d.  3d.  Pass Bye.
S. .. 8d.  6d.  5d.  4d.  3d.  Sarnau Road.
S. .. 9d.  7d.  6d.  5d.  4d.  3d.  Bankyfelin.
S. .. 10d. 8d.  7d.  6d.  5d.  4d.  3d.  Rushmoor.
S. .. 11d. 9d.  8d.  7d.  6d.  5d.  4d.  3d.  New Church.
S. .. 1/1  11d. 10d. 9d.  8d.  7d.  6d.  5d.  3d.  Upper St. Clears.
S. .. 1/3  1/1  1/-  11d. 10d. 9d.  8d.  7d.  6d.  4d.  Llanddowror.
S. .. 1/5  1/3  1/2  1/1  1/-  11d. 10d. 9d.  8d.  6d.  3d.  Tucking Mill.
S. .. 1/6  1/5  1/4  1/3  1/2  1/1  1/-  11d. 9d.  7d.  5d.  3d.  Quarry.
S. .. 1/7  1/6  1/5  1/4  1/3  1/2  1/1  1/-  10d. 9d.  6d.  5d.  Red Roses.
S. .. 1/10 1/9  1/8  1/7  1/6  1/5  1/4  1/2  1/1  1/-  10d. 8d.  Llanteg.
S. .. 2/-  1/10 1/9  1/8  1/7  1/6  1/5  1/4  1/2  1/1  11d. 9d.  Penybont.
S. .. 2/2  2/-  1/11 1/10 1/9  1/8  1/7  1/6  1/4  1/3  1/1  11d. Commercial.
S. .. 2/4  2/2  2/1  2/-  1/11 1/10 1/9  1/8  1/6  1/5  1/3  1/1  Stepaside.
S. .. 2/5  2/3  2/2  2/1  2/-  1/11 1/10 1/9  1/7  1/6  1/4  1/2  Kilgetty.
S. .. 2/6  2/4  2/3  2/2  2/1  2/-  1/11 1/10 1/8  1/7  1/5  1/3  Kingsmoor.
S. .. 2/7  2/5  2/4  2/3  2/2  2/1  2/-  1/11 1/10 1/8  1/6  1/4  Hill.
S. .. 2/8  2/6  2/5  2/4  2/3  2/2  2/1  2/-  1/11 1/9  1/7  1/5  Stonybridge.
S. .. 2/10 2/8  2/7  2/6  2/5  2/4  2/3  2/2  2/1  1/11 1/9  1/7  Saundersfoot Road.
S. .. 2/11 2/9  2/8  2/7  2/6  2/5  2/4  2/3  2/2  2/-  1/10 1/8  Brynhir.
S. .. 3/1  2/11 2/10 2/9  2/8  2/7  2/6  2/5  2/4  2/2  2/-  1/10 Tenby.
```

```
Quarry.
S. .. 4d.  Red Roses.
S. .. 7d.  4d.  Llanteg.
S. .. 8d.  7d.  4d.  Penybont.
S. .. 11d. 9d.  6d.  4d.  Commercial.
S. .. 1/-  11d. 8d.  6d.  4d.  Stepaside.
S. .. 1/1  1/-  9d.  7d.  5d.  3d.  Kilgetty.
S. .. 1/2  1/1  10d. 8d.  6d.  4d.  3d.  Kingsmoor.
S. .. 1/3  1/2  11d. 9d.  7d.  5d.  4d.  3d.  Hill.
S. .. 1/4  1/3  1/-  10d. 9d.  7d.  6d.  4d.  3d.  Stonybridge.
S. .. 1/6  1/5  1/2  1/-  10d. 8d.  7d.  6d.  5d.  4d.  Saundersfoot Road.
S. .. 1/7  1/6  1/3  1/1  11d. 9d.  8d.  7d.  6d.  5d.  3d.  Brynhir.
S. .. 1/9  1/8  1/5  1/4  1/1  11d. 10d. 8d.  7d.  6d.  4d.  3d.  Tenby.
```

Special Returns.

Carmarthen to Tenby, 4/-.

Ordinary Returns.

S.	R.	S.	R.	S.	R.	S.	R.
4d.	7d.	10d.	1/6	1/6	2/6	2/2	3/6
5d.	9d.	11d.	1/7	1/7	2/8	2/3	3/8
6d.	10d.	1/1	1/9	1/9	3/-	2/4	3/9
7d.	1/-	1/3	2/-	1/11	3/3	2/5	3/10
8d.	1/3	1/4	2/3	2/-	3/3	2/6	4/-
9d.	1/5	1/5	2/5	2/1	3/5		

….. continued on next page:

Continued:

Season tickets.—Monthly (unlimited) : 2/- per 1d. stage. Quarterly (unlimited) : 5/- per 1d. stage. Weekly tickets : One journey per day ; One service—6d. per 1d. stage ; Available both services—6d. per booking extra. School tickets.—Available only Monday to Friday : 3d. per 1d. stage per week. Apprentice tickets.—Not in excess of 10/- per week salary : 4d. per 1d. stage.

Children over 3 and under 14 years of age half fare, with minimum fare of 1d. Period tickets at cheap rates.

3563/6—Between Pendine and Tenby. Revised fare table :—

```
           Pendine.
S. ..  3d.   Llanmiloe.
S. ..  6d.   4d.   Brook.
S. ..  7d.   5d.   3d.   Plashett.
S. ..  8d.   6d.   4d.   3d.   Mansion.
S. ..  9d.   8d.   6d.   5d.   4d.   Laugharne.
S. ..  1/-   10d.  9d.   7d.   6d.   3d.   Cross Inn.
S. ..  1/1   11d.  10d.  8d.   7d.   5d.   3d.   Morfa Bach.
S. ..  1/2   1/-   11d.  9d.   8d.   7d.   5d.   3d.   Lower St. Clears.
S. ..  1/4   1/2   1/1   11d.  10d.  8d.   6d.   5d.   3d.   Upper St. Clears.
S. ..  1/3   1/1   1/-   11d.  10d.  9d.   8d.   7d.   6d.   4d.   Llanddowror.
S. ..  1/5   1/3   1/2   1/1   1/-   11d.  10d.  9d.   8d.   6d.   3d.   Tucking Mill.
S. ..  1/6   1/5   1/4   1/3   1/2   1/1   1/-   11d.  9d.   7d.   5d.   3d.   Quarry.
S. ..  1/7   1/6   1/5   1/4   1/3   1/2   1/1   1/-   10d.  9d.   6d.   5d.   3d.   Red Roses.
S. ..  1/10  1/9   1/8   1/7   1/6   1/5   1/4   1/2   1/1   1/-   10d.  8d.   Llanteg.
S. ..  2/-   1/10  1/9   1/8   1/7   1/6   1/5   1/4   1/2   1/1   11d.  9d.   Penybont.
S. ..  2/2   2/-   1/11  1/10  1/9   1/8   1/7   1/6   1/4   1/3   1/1   11d.  Commercial.
S. ..  2/4   2/2   2/1   2/-   1/11  1/10  1/9   1/8   1/6   1/5   1/3   1/1   Stepaside.
S. ..  2/5   2/3   2/2   2/1   2/-   1/11  1/10  1/9   1/7   1/6   1/4   1/2   Kilgetty.
S. ..  2/6   2/4   2/3   2/2   2/1   2/-   1/11  1/10  1/8   1/7   1/5   1/3   Kingsmoor.
S. ..  2/7   2/5   2/4   2/3   2/2   2/1   2/-   1/11  1/10  1/8   1/6   1/4   Hill.
S. ..  2/8   2/6   2/5   2/4   2/3   2/2   2/1   2/-   1/11  1/9   1/7   1/5   Stonybridge.
S. ..  2/10  2/8   2/7   2/6   2/5   2/4   2/3   2/2   2/1   1/11  1/9   1/7   Saundersfoot Road.
S. ..  2/11  2/9   2/8   2/7   2/6   2/5   2/4   2/3   2/2   2/-   1/10  1/8   Brynhir.
S  ..  3/1   2/11  2/10  2/9   2/8   2/7   2/6   2/5   2/4   2/2   2/-   1/10  Tenby.
           Quarry.
S. ..  4d.   Red Roses.
S. ..  7d.   4d.   Llanteg.
S. ..  8d.   7d.   4d.   Penybont.
S. ..  11d.  9d.   6d.   4d.   Commercial.
S. ..  1/-   11d.  8d.   6d.   4d.   Stepaside.
S. ..  1/1   1/-   9d.   7d.   5d.   3d.   Kilgetty.
S. ..  1/2   1/1   10d.  8d.   6d.   4d.   3d.   Kingsmoor.
S. ..  1/3   1/2   11d.  9d.   7d.   5d.   4d.   3d.   Hill.
S. ..  1/4   1/3   1/-   10d.  9d.   7d.   6d.   4d.   3d.   Stonybridge.
S. ..  1/6   1/5   1/2   1/-   10d.  8d.   7d.   6d.   5d.   4d.   Saundersfoot Road.
S. ..  1/7   1/6   1/3   1/1   11d.  9d.   8d.   7d.   6d.   5d.   3d.   Brynhir.
S. ..  1/9   1/8   1/5   1/4   1/1   11d.  10d.  8d.   7d.   6d.   4d.   3d.   Tenby.
```

Special Returns.

Pendine to Tenby, 4/-.   St. Clears to Tenby, 3/-.

Laugharne to Tenby, 3/6.

The setting down point of both services was Grey Garages' door, on South Parade, Tenby, and the picking up point was directly opposite the War Memorial on South Parade, Tenby.

Above: The second and last Leyland 'Titan' PD2/1 acquired by the company was **GBX 808**, which was licenced in June 1951. This was also bodied by Leyland Motors to L27/26R layout, and was pictured here in Lammas St, Carmarthen, working the Carmarthen - Tenby service in the summer of 1953. Just visible in the backdrop is the Royal Welsh Fusiliers Monument, with N & A Lloyd's newsagents shop, and The Colombo Bakery & Café on the left. *(Dr Michael A. Taylor).*

Above: Another view of the Leyland 'Titan' PD2/1, **GBX 808**, in Lammas Street, Carmarthen, but this time working the Pendine route, accompanied by stablemate TH 9010, another all Leyland 'Titan' TD5, which was working a summertime duplicate journey to the popular seaside village of Pendine. *(D.A.Jones. LTBPS).*

Above: The company's first underfloor engine vehicle was **GTH 956**, this Leyland 'Royal Tiger' PSU1/13, with Leyland B44F bodywork, delivered in May 1952, and followed 16 months later by another identical 'Royal Tiger'. *(The Leyland Society).*

Above: Another Leyland publicity photograph of 'Royal Tiger' **GTH 956**, taken before delivery. *(The Leyland Society).*

On 5th March, 1952, the company applied for modifications to all three stage carriage service licences, TGR 3563/1, 3563/2, and 3563/6, as follows:-

[1] Jointly with Williams Bros., to introduce revised weekly and season tickets as authorised to Western Welsh O.C., and other companies.

[2] To charge a booking fee of 6d, on tickets interchangeable with Williams Bros.

Condition [1] was granted, but condition [2] was refused, on 28th May, 1952.

Another modification asked for on 23rd July, 1952, was to operate four additional journeys in each direction on the summer timetable (1st May to 30th Sept), between Carmarthen and Tenby, TGR 3563/1. This application was objected to by Western Welsh O.C., Greens Motors Ltd., D.J. Morrison Ltd., and the Railway Executive (Western Region), which resulted in a public sitting at 'Shire Hall', Carmarthen, in September 1952, where the additional journeys were refused.

In March 1953, they asked for revision of the summer and winter timetable, on Carmarthen to Pendine (which ran in conjunction with Williams Bros. on alternate Sundays) as follows:-

The journey arriving Carmarthen (Lammas St) at 1.55 pm, to be extended to Carmarthen Hospital (Priory St), and thence to Glangwili Hospital, via King St, Priory St, and Old Oak. For passengers visiting both hospitals only. No extra fare to be charged for the extension. The application was withdrawn on 27th May, 1953, after objections from Western Welsh.

Three months later, on 8th July, 1953, a modification was asked for on TGR 3563/1. To divert the journey leaving Carmarthen at 9.00 am, by leaving the A477 at Railway Inn, Kilgetty, then along Kingsmoor Park Rd., to join A478 at Kingsmoor Head. Also to divert the journey leaving Tenby at 10.30 am, at Kilgetty, leaving A478 at Kingsmoor Head, then along Kingsmoor Park Rd, to join A477 at Railway Inn, Kilgetty. This amendment was granted on 30th September, 1953.

On 14th October, 1953, another new workmen's stage carriage licence was applied for:-

TGR 3563/11   **Mydrim to Pendine (M o S Experimental Establishment, Llanmilo).**
via: St Clears, Laugharne, and Llanmilo. *Mondays to Fridays.*
Only workmen employed at the Ministry of Supply Experimental Establishment to be carried on this service. Licence granted 17/2/1954.

The following special short term licences were issued to operate the above service:-

TGR 3563/Sp/1   Period of operation 21st September 1953 to 14th November 1953.

TGR 3563/Sp/2   "   "   "   16th November 1953 to 9th January 1954.

TGR 3563/Sp/3   "   "   "   11th January 1954 to 19th February 1954.

Above: JBX 220 was the second Leyland 'Royal Tiger' PSU1/13 in the Ebsworth Brothers fleet, and was identically bodied by Leyland Motors, to B44F layout. This one arrived in September 1953, and was sadly, the very last vehicle purchased by the partnership before the company's demise in December 1954. *(Courtesy of The Leyland Society).*

Above: Another Leyland Motors publicity photograph of Leyland 'Royal Tiger' JBX 220, which was taken before delivery to Laugharne, in September 1953. *(Courtesy of The Leyland Society).*

WEEK-DAY SERVICES THROUGHOUT THE YEAR.

PENDINE :: LAUGHARNE :: ST. CLEARS :: CARMARTHEN

WEEK-DAYS — Pendine → Carmarthen

Stop		a.m.	a.m.	a.m.	a.m.	p.m.	p.m.	p.m.	p.m.	p.m.	p.m.
Pendine	Dept.	7.15	7.45	10.00	12.00	2.00	4.00	6.0	8.0	10.00	12.0
Laugharne	,,		8.00	10.15	12.15	2.15	4.15	6.15	8.15	10.15	12.15
St. Clears	,,		8.15	10.25	12.25	2.25	4.25	6.25	8.25	10.25	
Banoyfelin	,,		8.25	10.35	12.35	2.35	4.35	6.35	8.35	10.35	
Pass-By	,,		8.30	10.40	12.40	2.40	4.40	6.40	8.40	10.40	
Carmarthen	Arr.	7.55	8.45	10.55	12.55	2.55	4.55	6.55	8.55	10.55	

WEEK-DAYS — Carmarthen → Pendine

Stop		a.m.	a.m.	a.m.	p.m.	p.m.	p.m.	p.m.	p.m.	p.m.
Carmarthen	Dept.	8.0	9.0	11.0	1.0	3.0	5.0	7.0	9.0	11.0
Pass-By	,,		9.15	11.15	1.15	3.15	5.15	7.15	9.15	11.15
Banoyfelin	,,		9.20	11.20	1.20	3.20	5.20	7.20	9.20	11.20
St. Clears	,,		9.25	11.25	1.25	3.25	5.25	7.25	9.25	11.25
Laugharne	,,		9.40	11.40	1.40	3.40	5.40	7.40	9.40	11.40
Pendine	Arr.	8.55	9.55	11.55	1.55	3.55	5.55	7.55	9.55	11.55

SUNDAY SERVICES—SUMMERTIME (First Sunday in May to Last Sunday in September)

Pendine → Carmarthen

Stop		a.m.	noon
Pendine	Dept.	10.0	12.0
Laugharne	,,	10.15	12.15
St. Clears	,,	10.25	12.25
Carmarthen	Arr.	10.55	12.55

Carmarthen → Pendine

Stop		a.m.	p.m.
Carmarthen	Dept.		9.0
St. Clears	,,		9.30
Laugharne	,,	9.40	10.0
Pendine	Arr.	9.55	10.10

SUNDAY SERVICES—WINTERTIME (First Sunday in October to Last Sunday in April).

Pendine → Carmarthen

Stop		p.m.	p.m.
Pendine	Dept.	1.0	4.0
Laugharne	,,	1.15	4.15
St. Clears	,,	1.25	4.25
Carmarthen	Arr.	1.55	4.55

Carmarthen → Pendine

Stop		p.m.	p.m.	p.m.	p.m.	p.m.
Carmarthen	Dept.		2.0	5.0	7.0	9.0
St. Clears	,,	12.40	2.25	5.25	7.25	9.25
Laugharne	,,		2.40	5.40	7.40	9.40
Pendine	Arr.	12.55	2.55	5.55	7.55	9.55

Please note that the above Wintertime Sunday Services will run alternate weeks by Messrs. Williams Brothers, Laugharne.

Returning to September 1951, Ebsworth Brothers' director and financier, Julian Stephen Hodge, became a director of Jeremy's Garages, Tenby, and in June 1952, transferred Ebsworth Bros.' Crossley coach, ETH 785, to the associate company, Jeremy's Garages, which was now included in the 'Hodge Group' of companies. However, Jeremy's Garages failed to get an operator's licence to run the coach due to an objection from D.J. Morrison, Tenby. The coach eventually returned to the Ebsworth Bros.' fleet, unused, in October 1953.

Julian S. Hodge was a director of numerous companies across South Wales and the West Country, and became a director of Jeremy's Garages (Haverfordwest) Ltd., in January 1953.

It was commonly known that Western Welsh harassed both Ebsworth Bros. and Williams Bros. WWOC continuously objected to their licence applications and licence renewals, so it was not a surprise when they once again objected to the licence renewals of Ebsworth Bros.' TGR 3563/2, and Williams Bros.' TGR 457/2, jointly operated Carmarthen to Pendine service in October 1953. It became the subject of another public hearing at 'Shire Hall', Carmarthen, on 17th February, 1954, where the licences were granted.

The last licence for workmen's unforeseen stage carriage service was issued in Nov. 1954:-

TGR 3563/Sp/4   **Carmarthen** to **Pendine (Ministry of Supply, P & EE, Llanmilo).**
Period of operation, 1/12/1954 to 5/12/1954 inclusive.

In the meantime, the company were in debt after buying so many new buses, and could not repay their hire purchase commitments to their financier/company director, Julian Hodge.

Mr Hodge wanted his money, so he offered the company to T.G. Davies, the General Manager of Western Welsh O.C., who was a former colleague of Julian Hodge at the GWR.

Western Welsh accepted the offer, and an agreement was made on 4th November, 1954 to purchase Ebsworth Bros.' eleven omnibuses and eleven services for £27,500. Premises were not included in the sale. The final agreement between both parties was drawn up, signed, sealed, and delivered, on 29th November, 1954.

In the meantime, Western Welsh had applied for all eleven Ebsworth Bros.' road service licences on 27th October, 1954.

Vendors listed on the Ebsworth Brothers agreement, dated 29th November, 1954, were:-

John Lewis Ebsworth, 'Rycroft' Narberth Road, Tenby.	Company director.
Lilian Edna Ebsworth, 'Rycroft' Narberth Road, Tenby.	Married woman.
William Mervyn Roberts, Elm House, King Street, Laugharne.	Manager.
Samuel Ernest Taylor, 2 Heol Gabriel, Whitchurch, Cardiff.	Accountant.
Ivor Morris, Highfield, Holloway, Tenby.	
John Ronald Taylor, Llandennis Ave., Cyncoed, Cardiff.	Company director.
Frederick Donald Walters, Alltmawr Road, Cyncoed, Cardiff.	Company director.
Julian Stephen Hodge, White Lodge, Ty-Gwyn Ave, Penylan, C'diff.	Accountant.

THE DEMISE OF EBSWORTH BROTHERS Ltd.

On Monday, 6th December, 1954, The Western Welsh Omnibus Co. Ltd., took control of the Ebsworth Bros. undertaking, swiftly discarding the name and livery. Eleven vehicles passed to Western Welsh with the business, along with all licences, services, contracts, and some of the staff. Ebsworth Bros.' premises at Laugharne were not acquired in the transaction, but alternatively, a parking area opposite Ebsworth Bros.' garage in Clifton Street, Laugharne, large enough to house six buses, was rented from R. Edmunds, Easthill, Laugharne, initially for £13 per quarter (£1.0.0. per week). No facilities were provided at this yard which was registered as an outstation to Carmarthen depot.

The Stage Carriage, Express Carriage, Excursion & Tours licences acquired from Ebsworth Bros on 6th December, 1954, were:-

3563/1	Carmarthen to Tenby via: St Clears/Red Roses, which became		TGR 441/639
3563/2	Carmarthen to Pendine via: Laugharne.	"	TGR 441/640
3563/3	Excursions & Tours starting from Laugharne.	"	TGR 441/646
3563/4	Excursions & Tours starting from St Clears.	"	TGR 441/647
3563/5	Excursions & Tours starting from Carmarthen (Lammas St)	"	TGR 441/648
3563/6	Pendine to Tenby via: Laugharne & St Clears.	"	TGR 441/641
3563/7	Excursions & Tours starting from Pendine (Beach Hotel).	"	TGR 441/649
3563/8	St Clears to Pendine (MoS workers).	"	TGR 441/642
3563/9	Laugharne to Pendine (MoS workers).	"	TGR 441/643
3563/10	Carmarthen to Pendine (MoS workers).	"	TGR 441/644
3563/11	Mydrim to Pendine (MoS workers)	"	TGR 441/645

Ebsworth Bros.' road service licences, TGR 3563/1 to TGR 3563/11 were all surrendered by February 1955.

Vehicles transferred to WWOC were:- Leyland TD5 - TH 9010, Leyland PD1A - CTH 828, Crossley SD42/7 - ETH 785, Dennis Lance - FBX 35, Leyland PD2/1 - FTH 445/GBX 808, Leyland PS1/1 - FBX 491/FBX 754/JHA 261, Leyland PSU1/13 - GTH 956/JBX 220.

<u>Note:</u> TH 9010 was given Western Welsh f/n 984 but did not operate with them.

After the business passed to Western Welsh, John Lewis Ebsworth (Jack) went into retirement, and later moved house, to live at 43 Heol Iscoed, Whitchurch, Cardiff. He was still residing there when he passed away at St Mary's Hospital, Paddington, London, on 1st November, 1960, aged 66.

His brother David Lewis Ebsworth, remained as manager of Clifton Garage, after the sale of the omnibus business, and was still living at Clifton House, Laugharne, when he passed away on 21st February, 1956, aged 75. The youngest brother, Harold Victor Ebsworth, passed away in 1970, aged 72.

Above: When Western Welsh O.C. absorbed Ebsworth Brothers' omnibus business in December 1954, they did not acquire the depot, Clifton Garage. That was retained by the Ebsworth family as a motor repair garage and petrol filling station, which included motor car sales. Western Welsh decided that their Laugharne operation could easily be operated as an outstation from their Carmarthen depot, and a suitable plot of land was sought after. This photograph depicts the rented plot of land in Clifton Street, opposite Clifton Garage, which was initially rented for £13 per quarter (£1.0.0 per week), and was large enough to house 6 buses. These two Leyland 'Tiger Cubs' 306 CUH (1306) and SBO 247 (1247) were regular performers on the former Ebsworth Bros.' Carmarthen – Pendine route, which became Western Welsh service 411, together with PBO 687 (687), the AEC Bridgemaster, only partially visible in the back of the yard. *(V. Morgan collection).*

Above: After Ebsworth Bros. were absorbed by Western Welsh, their Davies bodied Dennis 'Lance III', **FBX 35**, became the only 'Lance' in the WWOC fleet. It received f/n 983, and was transferred to Cardiff, where it's seen here. *(Geoff Morant).*

Above: Former Ebsworth Bros.' Leyland PD2/1 'Titan', **FTH 445**, received f/n 981 with WWOC, and is seen here outside the Golden Lion Hotel, Lammas St, Carmarthen, working a Western Welsh service to Llanstephan and Llanybri. *(The Bus Archive).*

Above: This former Ebsworth Bros.' Leyland 'Titan' PD2/1, **GBX 808,** received f/n 942 at Western Welsh. *(Roy Marshall).*

Above: Pictured here at Lammas Street, Carmarthen, is former Ebsworth Bros. **GTH 956**, a Leyland 'Royal Tiger' PSU1/13, with Leyland B44F bodywork, which had just arrived from Pendine and Laugharne. However, I must say, the conductress looks rather mystified! She is so engrossed in what's going on, she's not helping the aged to alight. This Royal Tiger received WWOC f/n 470, and finished up working for a contractor at Barrhead, in Scotland. *(V. Morgan collection).*

Above: Leyland 'Royal Tiger' **JBX 220**, however, got shipped off to Bridgend to work for Western Welsh, receiving f/n 471.
(Alan Cross).

Above: Western Welsh AEC 'Bridgemaster' 687, **PBO 687**, normally worked the Carmarthen – Pendine route, but is photographed here, parked up at Carmarthen depot, between duties on the Pendine service. *(V. Morgan collection).*

Above: This Western Welsh, Willowbrook bodied Leyland 'Tiger Cub', **MKG 479** (1479), was working the former Ebsworth Bros.' route between Pendine and Carmarthen, when it was captured outside the 'Spring Well' public house at Pendine, having made its reverse manoeuver, ready for the return journey to Carmarthen. *(Alan Broughall).*

Above: An earlier view of Western Welsh (1479), seen at Laugharne outstation in dual purpose livery. *(V. Morgan collection).*

VEHICLE DETAILS - EBSWORTH BROS. Ltd.

Reg No	Chassis Make & Type	Chassis number	Body make & type	Seating	Date New	Remarks / Additional Information Previous Owner	Date Acquired	Date Withdrawn
BX 164	Beaufort 24hp u/w 24 cwt		Interchangeable bodies Touring/Wagon			Possibly second-hand. Registered 7/11/1910 to J.S. Ebsworth, Sea View, Pendine.	11/1910	?
BX 737	Ford 'T' 20hp		Taxi	5	2/1916	Registered new to D.L. Ebsworth, Beach Hotel, Pendine, 11/2/1916.	2/1916	?
BX 897	Puritan 'Lyon' 20/30hp		Laundaulette, rebuilt into a bus by the brothers.	originally 5 seats	3/1919	Ex Dd Williams, 14 Railway Tce, Llanelly. Reg to Ebsworth Bros, Fullerton House, Laugharne.	5/1919	?
BX	Austin 2-Shaft		Austin		?	Named: 'The Pearl'.	1919	?
BX 1021	Ford 'T' 20hp				10/1919	New. Licensed to carry passengers.	10/1919	?
BX 1114	Traffic 20-25hp u/w 30cwt.		Lorry		2/1920	New. Licensed to D.L. Ebsworth.	2/1920	?
BX 1135	Ford 'T' 20hp			5	2/1920	Ex Benjamin Davies, County Stores, St Clears. Licensed to carry passengers.	3/1920	?
BX 1260	Traffic 20-25hp u/w 30cwt.		S. Jackett & Sons, Coachbuilders, Llanelly.	Charabanc	24/4/1920	New (colour, French Grey).	4/1920	?
BX 1432	Ford 'T' 20hp u/w 14cwt				8/1920	New	8/1920	?
BX 235-	Oldsmobile			B- -R			?	?
BX 6628	Dodge			B- F	3/1926	New	1/3/1926	?
BX 7757	Lancia Pentaiota			B- F	4/1927	New	4/1927	?
BX 8540	Leyland PLSC3 u/w 4t 15cwt	46672	C.K. Andrews. Swansea.	B32-	4/1928	New (colour, chocolate + brown)	4/1928	7/1940
BX 9719	Star 'Flyer' VB4 3 ton chassis	VB1104	Star	B26-	18/4/1929	New	licenced 5/1929	1933
TH 617	Chevrolet 30cwt chassis	65386		B14F	4/1930	New	16/4/1930	?

185

Reg	Make/Model	No.	Body	Code	Date	Note	Date	Date
TH 618	Leyland 'Tiger' TS2 u/w 4t 16cwt	60974	Thomas & Thomas	B32F	5/1930	New	9/5/1930	7/1940
TH 1725	Morris 'Viceroy' YB6 u/w 3t 7cwt 1qr	268Y	Thomas & Thomas	B26D	5/1931	New	5/1931	1938
TH 2574	Leyland 'Bull' TSQ3 u/w 5t 12cwt 1qr		Tipper lorry		5/1932	New	6/1932	?
TH 2901	Leyland		Lorry		11/1932	New	11/1932	?
TH 3333	Leyland 'Tiger' TS4	2692	Thomas & Thomas	B35D	4/1933	New Registered to T.L. Ebsworth.	4/1933	1950
TH 4908	Leyland		Lorry		11/1934	New	11/1934	?
TH 5515	Leyland 'Tiger' TS7 oil u/w 5ton	6384		35	6/1935	New	6/1935	6/1950
TH 7062	Leyland		Lorry		5/1936	New	5/1936	?
TH 9010	Leyland 'Titan' TD5 oil u/w 6t 10cwt	14723	Leyland	L27/26R	7/1937	New	7/1937	12/1954
ABX 230	unknown lorry				5/1938	New	5/1938	?
ABX 231	unknown lorry				5/1938	New	5/1938	?
ABX 467	Bedford WTB u/w 3ton	112362	Duple	C26F	7/1938	New	7/1938	11/1950
ATH 782	Rover 12		Car		5/1939	New	7/1938	?
ATH 783	International		Lorry		5/1939	New	5/1939	?
ATH 784	International		Lorry		5/1939	New	5/1939	?
ATH 785	International		Lorry		5/1939	New	5/1939	?
ATH 786	International		Lorry		5/1939	New	5/1939	?

ATH 787	International		Lorry		5/1939	New	5/1939	?
ATH 788	International		Lorry		5/1939	New	5/1939	?
WJ 9093	Leyland 'Titan' TD3c oil engine/manual g-box	3605	Cravens Railway-Carriage and Wagon Co.	H31/24R	1/1934	Ex Sheffield C.T (A93), via W Alexander, Falkirk (R324, not operated), through Millburn (dealer).	11/1942	6/1953
CBX 188	Bedford		Lorry		12/1943	New	12/1943	?
GJ 7537	Leyland 'Titan' TD1	71395	Burlingham (1945)	H29/25R	6/1930	Ex Premier Omnibus Co. London (see p161 for more info) via J. Green, Brierley Hill, Staffs.	5/1946	by 1951
CTH 828	Leyland 'Titan' PD1A u/w 7t 0c 1qr	462243	Leyland	L27/26R	12/1946	New	1/1947	12/1954
BDW 13	Leyland 'Tiger' TS8	14619	Weymann	B36F	8/1937	Ex Newport Corporation Transport (60). via Corvedale Motors, Ludlow, Salop. (15).	1948	by 3/1953
ETH 785 see below	Crossley SD42/7 u/w 6t 8c 3qr	97912	D.J. Davies	C33F	4/1949	New	4/1949	6/1952 see below
FBX 35	Dennis 'Lance III'	108K3	D.J. Davies	H30/26R	6/1949	New	7/1949	12/1954
FBX 491	Leyland 'Tiger' PS1/1	492042	D.J. Davies	C33F	9/1949	New	9/1949	12/1954
FBX 754	Leyland 'Tiger' PS1/1	493312	D.J. Davies	DP35F	1/1950	New	1/1950	12/1954
FTH 445	Leyland 'Titan' PD2/1	501191	Leyland	L27/26R	6/1950	New	6/1950	12/1954
GBX 808	Leyland 'Titan' PD2/1	502182	Leyland	L27/26R	5/1951	New	5/1951	12/1954
GTH 956	Leyland 'Royal Tiger' PSU1/13	520908	Leyland	B44F	5/1952	New	5/1952	12/1954
JHA 261	Leyland 'Tiger' PS1/1	461166	Harrington	C33F	10/1946	Ex Gliderways. Smethwick, Staffs (19). via K.P. John (Kenfig Motors), Kenfig Hill. Glam.	1/1953	12/1954
JBX 220	Leyland 'Royal Tiger' PSU1/13	531591	Leyland	B44F	9/1953	New	9/1953	12/1954
ETH 785 See above	Crossley SD42/7	97912	D.J. Davies	C33F	4/1949	Re-acquired from an associate company, Jeremy's Garages, Tenby.	10/1953	12/1954

VEHICLE DISPOSALS - EBSWORTH BROS. Ltd

BX 164	No further trace.
BX 737	No further trace.
BX 897	No further trace.
BX - - -	(Austin 2 shaft) No further trace.
BX 1021	No further trace.
BX 1114	No further trace.
BX 1135	To unknown owner at Hereford.
BX 1260	To unknown Swansea owner, later to Pembrokeshire.
BX 235 -	No further trace.
BX 6628	No further trace.
BX 7757	No further trace.
BX 8540	Requisitioned by the Ministry of War Transport, for Royal Air Force in 7/1940. Not returned.
BX 9719	Last licensed 1933. No further trace.
TH 617	The body was advertised for sale on 23/5/1933, in good condition, as new, cheap. The chassis was converted into a lorry by 12/1935.
TH 618	Requisitioned by the Ministry of War Transport, for Royal Air Force in 7/1940. Scrapped 2/1944.
TH 1725	Last licensed 1938. No further trace.
BX 2574	No further trace.
TH 2901	No further trace.
TH 3333	Last licensed 1950. Derelict by 8/1951.
TH 5515	Sold to C. Davies. Pontlottyn, Glam, 9/1950.
TH 7062	No further trace.
TH 9010	To Western Welsh (984), with the business 12/1954. Not used by WWOC. Sold to South Wales Motor Traders (dealer) Chepstow, 6/1956. No further trace.
ABX 230	No further trace.
ABX 231	No further trace.
ABX 467	Sold to Arthur Leyshon Jenkins, Laugharne (an Ebsworth Bros employee) & converted into a mobile Fish & Chip shop, which was a regular visitor to Pendine Sands. Pictured opposite.
ATH 782	No further trace.
ATH 783	No further trace.
ATH 784	No further trace.
ATH 785	No further trace.
ATH 786	No further trace.
ATH 787	No further trace.
ATH 788	No further trace.
WJ 9093	Certificate of Fitness expired 6/1953. No further trace.
CBX 188	No further trace.
GJ 7537	Sold to Williams Bros (Pioneer), Laugharne by 8/1951. To Lansdowne, Leytonstone, London E11, 6/1955, licensed by them 7/1955.
CTH 828	To Western Welsh (980), with the business 12/1954. To Coppock (dealer), Sale, Lancs, 3/1959. To Robinson, Wigan, Lancs, 4/1959.
BDW 13	Sold to T.M. Morris. Pencoed, Glam, for spares, 3/1953.
ETH 785	Transferred to associate company, Jeremy's Garages, Tenby, Pembs, 6/1952. (See notes page 163). Returned in 10/1953. Sold to Western Welsh (573), with the business 12/1954. No further trace.
FBX 35	To Western Welsh (983), with the business 12/1954. To Pentyrch Spastics Hospital, Cardiff, 5/1958, less engine.
FBX 491	To Western Welsh (571), with the business 12/1954. To Howells & Withers, Pontllanfraith, 5/1958, less engine & gearbox. To Morlais. Merthyr Tydfil, 8/1958, body fitted to EU 8610.
FBX 754	To Western Welsh (572), with the business 12/1954. To Howells & Withers, Pontllanfraith, 5/1958, less engine & gearbox. To Morlais, Merthyr Tydfil, 8/1958.
FTH 445	To Western Welsh (981), with the business 12/1954. To Jones (breaker) Cardiff, less engine, 3/1959.

GBX 808	To Western Welsh (982), with the business 12/1954. To F. Cowley (dealer), Salford, 9/1963. To Price, Romsley, Worcestershire, 12/1963.
GTH 956	To Western Welsh (470), with the business 12/1954. To F. Cowley (dealer), Salford, 7/1965. To Leggatt (contractor), Barrhead, East Renfrewshire, by 2/1966.
JHA 261	To Western Welsh (570), with the business 12/1954. To Howells & Withers, Pontllanfraith, 5/1958, less engine, body removed and fitted to EDM 325 of H & W.
JBX 220	To Western Welsh (471), with the business 12/1954. To F.Cowley (dealer) Salford, 9/1965. To McKeown, (contractor), Ballymena (NI) 11/1968.

Above: When Ebsworth Bros. withdrew this Duple bodied Bedford WTB, **ABX 467**, from service in November 1950, it was quickly snapped up by one of their employees, driver Arthur Jenkins of Laugharne. Ably assisted by his brother, they converted the coach into a mobile fish & chip shop, which is pictured at Pendine sands in the 1950's, doing a brisk business in front of the famous Beach Hotel. *(Courtesy of Peter 'Chips' Jenkins).*

PHOTOGRAPH INDEX - EBSWORTH BROS. Ltd

TICKETS USED BY EBSWORTH BROS.

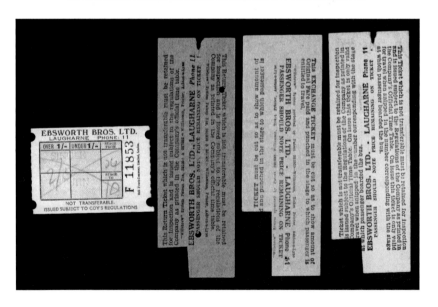

The bottom left ticket is a post WW2 'Bellgraphic' from 'Bell Punch Co'. All other tickets are the company's original antiquated 'Willebrew' ticket system, where the conductor cut a section out of the ticket so that the part issued to the passenger, displayed the fare paid. A time consuming task at the end of a shift, totalling up the amount payable.

Above: This 4 shillings and sixpence return ticket would have been issued for a return journey between Carmarthen and Tenby, shortly before the company's demise in 1954.

This completes the story of "The Laugharne Rivals" which is a great story of enterprise and achievement. Both families eventually settled their differences, and became good friends.